Real Food
from your
Slo-cooker

Real Food from your Slo-cooker

Annette Yates and Wendy Hobson

foulsham

LONDON • NEW YORK • TORONTO • SYDNEY

foulsham

The Publishing House, Bennetts Close,
Cippenham, Berks, SL1 5AP

ISBN 0-572-02536-X

Copyright © 1993 and 1999 W. Foulsham & Co. Ltd.

Some of these recipes also appear in *Tower Slo Cookbook*.

Cover photograph © Food Features.

Printed in Great Britain by Cox & Wyman Ltd., Reading, Berks.

CONTENTS

INTRODUCTION

For those of us with no time to spend cooking when we get home from work, slo-cookers fit perfectly into our busy lifestyles. Just prepare the ingredients and place them in your slo-cooker before leaving home and return to a delicious hot meal. Plus the meals are ready when you are; because of the time range, there is little chance of them spoiling even if you are an hour or two late.

A slo-cooker can be used day or night; cook tomorrow's lunch or breakfast overnight, for example. Use the slo-cooker while you are out, or while you are at home, and appreciate both the freedom of knowing that a delicious and nutritious meal is cooking itself and the satisfaction of economising on fuel. Some of the recipes have all-day cooking times, but others have shorter cooking times for a mid-day meal or when you simply want to get on with something more interesting!

Your slo-cooker also makes an ideal companion to your freezer as it is simple to use it for larger quantities than usual, then freeze some to use at a later date.

The following recipes provide a selection of interesting and tasty ideas for your slo-cooker. But don't stop there: use the recipes as a basis to experiment and develop your own favourite ideas so that your range of delicious meals never stops expanding.

CHOOSING A SLO-COOKER

Always choose a cooker that bears the BEAB safety symbol. Some older slo-cookers had a fixed pot, but most newer models have a removable pot for ease of use. All slo-cookers should have a well-fitting lid, which will be either heat-resistant glass or stoneware. It is not necessarily an advantage to have a glass lid as the condensation will block your view of the cooking food anyway. The heat settings available are High and Low, and some slo-cookers also have an automatic function

Choose a slo-cooker with sufficient capacity for your specific needs and consider whether you will use it for entertaining or for making extra quantities for the freezer. If you regularly cook for one, then a smaller capacity will be fine, but if you cook for four or more, own a freezer or entertain on a regular basis, look for a 3 litre/5¼ pt capacity. A cooker with a wide bowl will be easier to use for ingredients such as (bell) peppers, fish or whole fruit.

ADVANTAGES OF SLO-COOKING

There are many advantages to slo-cooking, especially for those who have better things to do than slave over a hot stove! Saving time may be top of your list of advantages, or perhaps the flexibility to cook when you want to and have a hot meal ready whenever you want to eat, but there are plenty of other positive features of slo-cooking.

Slo-cookers are superb for preparing soups, stocks, casseroles and stews. Flavours blend and develop to produce concentrated, rich and tasty results as all the flavours are sealed in the pot. The slow cooking method tenderises even the toughest cuts of meat and prevents shrinkage of joints.

You are not only saving time and effort but there are also considerable fuel economies with this cooking method. Fuel savings alone can be as much as 80 per cent on normal cooking times. The efficient built-in insulation means only the food inside the slo-cooker heats up, not the whole kitchen.

The gentle heat results in less evaporation of liquids so there is little chance of food drying out. The steam condenses on the lid and returns to the pot. In doing so it forms a seal that retains heat and flavour, which avoids steaming up the kitchen and filling it with cooking smells, losing valuable nutrients, and having to top up the steaming water for puddings! This makes the slo-cooker ideal for cooking light sponges and steaming smooth pâtés.

Foods cooked in the slo-cooker remain attractively whole – a distinct advantage when cooking fruit, fish and other ingredients. There is no need to turn or stir the food as it is not likely to overcook, boil over or stick and there are no hot spots to cause burning.

Once cooking is complete, food can safely be kept on the low setting for several hours without spoiling – making it perfect for families who do not all want to eat their meal at the same time.

PREPARATION & COOKING

A lways follow the manufacturer's instructions carefully when connecting the slo-cooker to the power supply. The appliance must be earthed. As different models will vary slightly, always check your instruction booklet for the usage instructions of your particular cooker. These basic rules are appropriate to all types of slo-cooker.

PREPARING FOOD

Always thaw frozen ingredients at room temperature before cooking.

Vegetables take longer to cook than meat as they normally cook at higher temperatures. They should therefore be thinly sliced or diced into 5 mm/¼ in pieces and placed near the bottom of the slo-cooker (the hottest point), covered in the cooking liquid. If you are browning the meat for a recipe, sauté the vegetables for a few minutes at the same time. Completely thaw frozen vegetables, then add them during the final hour of cooking.

Use quick-cooking varieties of pasta or rice and add to the dish for the last 30 minutes of cooking. Soften macaroni and lasagne in boiling water for a few minutes before cooking and make sure they are immersed in liquid. Extra liquid is needed when using raw rice: use 150 ml/¼ pt/⅔ cup for 100 g/4 oz/ ½ cup of rice. No additional liquid is required when slo-cooking cooked rice.

If using dried beans, soak them overnight in cold water, then bring to the boil in fresh water and boil rapidly for 15 minutes before draining and using in the recipe. This will destroy any natural toxins found in the beans.

Use seasoning and flavouring ingredients sparingly as most of their flavour is retained during cooking. If in doubt, season lightly, then adjust the seasoning of the finished dish.

USING YOUR SLO-COOKER

① Preheat the slo-cooker if necessary, with the lid on. You can prepare and brown the ingredients while the slo-cooker is heating.

② Browning ingredients before placing them in the slo-cooker can improve the appearance of the finished dish. Fry (sauté) prepared meat in a little oil in a frying pan (skillet) until browned, then add the prepared vegetables and fry until softened and starting to brown.

③ If you are using thickening agents, such as flour or cornflour (cornstarch), toss the pieces of meat in the flour before adding them to the frying pan, or stir them into the browning ingredients and stir until browned. If you have not added a thickening agent at the start of cooking, mix the flour or cornflour with a little cold water and stir it into the ingredients for the final 1–1½ hours of cooking.

④ Transfer the ingredients to the slo-cooker using a slotted spoon so that they come to within 1–2 cm/½–¾ in of the top of the earthenware pot. Stir in any seasonings.

⑤ Never leave uncooked food in the slo-cooker to be switched on later or store a removable slo-cooker pot in the fridge. If necessary, store prepared ingredients in a separate container in the fridge.

⑥ Always mix ingredients together well to prevent foods from sticking together.

⑦ Replace the lid and select the recommended heat setting. Where recipes recommend cooking on High for 20–30 minutes before turning to Low, you can use the Auto setting instead, if available.

⑧ Leave the slo-cooker undisturbed during the cooking period and keep the lid on, otherwise the water seal around the rim will be broken and a considerable time will be taken to regain the lost heat.

⑨ Stir soups and casseroles well before serving.

⑩ Once cooking is completed and the servings for that occasion have been used, transfer any remaining food from the slo-cooker, cool quickly, then chill or freeze.

ONE-STEP SLO-COOKING

In the one-step method, the cold ingredients are placed directly into the slo-cooker. You can use this method if you prefer not to brown food or if you are short of preparation time.

① Always preheat the slo-cooker.

② Make sure that vegetables are diced finely and place them in the slo-cooker before adding the meat or poultry and seasoning ingredients, then pour over enough boiling water to cover all the ingredients.

③ Mix the thickening agent with a little cold water to form a paste and stir in with the ingredients. Alternatively, coat the meat with flour before adding it to the slo-cooker. When the thickening agent is tomato purée (paste) or condensed soup, ensure these are mixed well with the other ingredients.

④ Add at least 3 hours on Low to recipe times if you are cooking by the one-step method. Recipes not suitable for one-step cooking are marked ①.

HINTS & TIPS

◇ Heat settings can often be adjusted to suit your lifestyle. Generally, the cooking time on High is just over half that on Low.

◇ Steamed dishes, recipes that include a raising agent and recipes with large pieces of meat should always be cooked on High.

◇ If steaming a pudding in a bowl or basin, fold a strip of foil and place it underneath the basin, then fold the strip over the top. When the pudding is finished, you will more easily be able to lift out the basin using the strip of foil.

◇ Avoid direct draughts and low room temperatures while cooking as these will affect the slo-cooker. Allow slightly longer cooking times if the room is likely to be cold, especially when cooking on Low.

◇ Recipe cooking times can be affected by variations in electricity supply. If the recipe is not ready at the end of the cooking time, replace the lid and cook for at least another hour on High.

◇ Cooked food should not be reheated in the slo-cooker.

◇ Add milk and cream to savoury dishes during the final 30 minutes since long cooking could cause them to separate.

◇ If your slo-cooker has a removable pot, cooked dishes can be browned under the grill (broiler) or covered with a topping and crisped in a preheated oven.

◇ Add dumplings to soups or stews for the final 30 minutes and switch to the High setting.

◇ Dry cooking is not advisable since it could damage your slo-cooker.

◇ If portions are to be eaten by latecomers, leave them in the slo-cooker on Low.

◇ Remember that the temperature of a slo-cooker on High does not compare with even the lowest setting in a conventional oven, so be careful when adapting conventional recipes. When adapting recipes for slo-cooking, use about half the normal quantity of liquid since there is less evaporation.

◇ Food that is not to be eaten straight away should always be cooled quickly before chilling or freezing. The slo-cooker will retain heat for some time, so do not leave food in the slo-cooker.

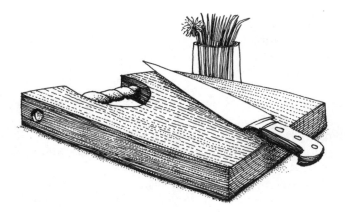

NOTES ON THE RECIPES

◇ All the recipes have been tested in a range of slo-cookers. However, models do vary, so it is a good idea to compare the cooking time of a recipe with a similar one in your own manufacturer's instruction book.

◇ Do not mix metric, imperial and American measures. Follow one set only.

◇ American terms are given in brackets.

◇ All spoon measurements are level: 1 tsp = 5 ml;
$\qquad\qquad\qquad\qquad\qquad\qquad$ 1 tbsp = 15 ml.

◇ Eggs are medium unless otherwise stated. If you use a different size, adjust the amount of liquid added to obtain the right consistency.

◇ Always wash, peel, core and seed, if necessary, fresh foods before use.

◇ Seasoning and the use of strongly flavoured ingredients, such as onions and garlic, is very much a matter of personal taste. Slo-cooked recipes tend to need less seasoning as the flavour is concentrated, so taste the food and adjust the seasoning as necessary.

◇ Always use fresh herbs unless dried are specifically called for. If you wish, you can substitute dried for fresh, using only half the quantity or less as they are very pungent, but chopped frozen varieties are much better than dried. There is no substitute for fresh parsley and coriander (cilantro).

◇ Use any good-quality oil, like sunflower, corn or groundnut (peanut), unless olive oil is called for.

◇ A fresh bouquet garni is traditionally made up of sprigs of thyme, parsley and a bay leaf tied together with string or wrapped in muslin (cheesecloth) and is used in slow-cooked dishes. Sachets of dried bouquet garni are readily available in supermarkets.

◇ Use butter or a margarine of your choice in the recipes. Since some margarines or spreads are best for particular uses, check the packet before using for the first time.

◇ Use your own discretion in substituting ingredients and personalising the recipes. Make notes of particular successes as you go along.

◇ Use whichever kitchen gadgets you like to speed up preparation and cooking times: mixers for whisking, food processors for grating, slicing, mixing or kneading, blenders for liquidising.

◇ Cooking times are approximate. If you alter the quantities of the recipe, the cooking times will vary only slightly because of the nature of the cooking method.

◇ Follow the preheating instructions for your own model of slo-cooker. Preheat your slo-cooker while you are preparing the ingredients.

◇ Serving suggestions are ideas only – use your own imagination!

RECIPE RATINGS

✖ Recipe is easy to prepare.

⚠ Recipe needs a little extra care during part or all of the preparation.

❄ Recipe is suitable for freezing.

⓪ Recipe should **not** be prepared by the one-step method.

SOUPS & STARTERS

Ideal for the slo-cooker, there's no worries about leaving your home-made soups for a few hours longer than the recommended cooking time. The results will still be delicious, perfectly cooked and tasty, the flavours from each ingredient having developed and intermingled gently for hours. The soups included in this section can be served as substantial starters, or accompanied by some crusty bread to make a meal in themselves.

If you can, use your leftover vegetables and bones to make stock in your slo-cooker, as it will be concentrated and full of flavour and will make the perfect base for soups, stews and casseroles.

The gentle heat of the slo-cooker is perfect for cooking pâtés, making them firm with a smooth texture and a delicate blend of flavours. They freeze well too, and are best if cut into individual servings and interleaved with foil or greaseproof (waxed) paper and over-wrapped with foil before freezing. Simply defrost at room temperature and they will be ready to serve.

SOUP TIPS

◇ Remember that vegetables take longer to cook than meat so should be finely diced.

◇ Browning the ingredients before slo-cooking will add extra flavour and colour to the finished soup.

◇ Season with care, and preferably after cooking, as slo-cooked soups retain more of their own concentrated flavours and therefore require less seasoning.

◇ If you use flour or cornflour (cornstarch) to thicken soups, add them at the start of cooking or for the final 1½ hours (see page 11).

◇ If you are using cream, milk or egg yolks to thicken a soup, add them for only the last 30 minutes of cooking.

◇ Use a good-quality chicken or vegetable stock.

◇ There is very little loss of liquid during cooking, so when adapting your own recipes, halve the amount of liquid added. You can also top up with boiling water once the dish is ready.

◇ Freeze cold soup in sealed polythene containers. Stock can be frozen in ice-cube bags so you can use it in small quantities when you need it in your cooking.

STOCK

—— MAKES ABOUT 1.75 LITRES/3 PTS/7½ CUPS ——

✗ ❄

	METRIC	IMPERIAL	AMERICAN
Raw or cooked bones or poultry carcass	1.75 kg	4 lb	4 lb
Onion, chopped	1	1	1
Carrot, chopped	1	1	1
Celery stick, chopped	1	1	1
Salt and whole black peppercorns			
Bouquet garni sachet	1	1	1
Boiling water			

① Preheat the slo-cooker on High.

② Break up the bones as small as possible to extract the most flavour. Place all the ingredients in the slo-cooker with sufficient boiling water to cover. Cook on Low for 10–16 hours.

③ Discard the bouquet garni. Strain the stock and leave to cool.

④ Skim off any surface fat and chill or freeze.

Freezing tip: Freeze in small quantities ready for use.

BEEF BROTH

—— SERVES 6–8 ——

	METRIC	IMPERIAL	AMERICAN
Oil	15 ml	1 tbsp	1 tbsp
Stewing steak, finely chopped	225 g	8 oz	8 oz
Onions, diced	2	2	2
Carrots, diced	225 g	8 oz	8 oz
Potatoes, diced	225 g	8 oz	8 oz
Leek, thinly sliced	1	1	1
Plain (all-purpose) flour	20 ml	4 tsp	4 tsp
Beef stock	1.2 litres	2 pts	5 cups
Pearl barley	25 g	1 oz	1 oz
Salt and freshly ground black pepper			

① Preheat the slo-cooker on High.

② Heat the oil in a frying pan (skillet) and fry (sauté) the meat gently until browned on all sides. Transfer to the slo-cooker.

③ Add the vegetables to the pan and fry gently for 3–4 minutes.

④ Stir in the flour, then gradually add the stock, stirring well. Add the pearl barley and seasoning. Bring to the boil, then transfer to the slo-cooker and stir well.

⑤ Cook on Low for 6–10 hours.

⑥ Stir well and adjust the seasoning before serving.

CHICKEN BROTH

—— SERVES 6–8 ——

Prepare as for Beef Broth, but substitute chicken meat and stock for the beef.

—— COOKING TIME: **LOW 6–10 HOURS** ——

SPLIT PEA SOUP

—— SERVES 6–8 ——

✄ ❄ ①

	METRIC	IMPERIAL	AMERICAN
Split peas	225 g	8 oz	1⅓ cups
Bicarbonate of soda (baking soda)	5 ml	1 tsp	1 tsp
Butter or margarine	25 g	1 oz	2 tbsp
Streaky bacon rashers (slices), rinded and chopped	4	4	4
Leek, chopped	1	1	1
Celery stick, chopped	1	1	1
Chicken stock	1 litre	1¾ pts	4¼ cups
Dried mixed herbs	5 ml	1 tsp	1 tsp
Salt and freshly ground black pepper			

① Soak the split peas in plenty of cold water with the bicarbonate of soda for 5–6 hours or overnight.

② Preheat the slo-cooker on High.

③ Heat the butter or margarine in a frying pan (skillet) and fry (sauté) the bacon, leek and celery for 3–4 minutes. Transfer to the slo-cooker.

④ Strain the split peas, then stir them into the slo-cooker with the stock and herbs. Season with salt and pepper.

⑤ Cook on Low for 8–10 hours.

⑥ Purée or mash the soup, then reheat before serving.

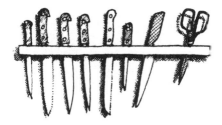

—— COOKING TIME: **LOW 8–10 HOURS** ——

FRENCH ONION SOUP

—— SERVES 6 ——

✗ ✻	METRIC	IMPERIAL	AMERICAN
Butter or margarine	40 g	1½ oz	3 tbsp
Onions, thinly sliced	700 g	1½ lb	1½ lb
Chicken stock	1 litre	1¾ pts	4¼ cups
Bay leaf	1	1	1
Salt and freshly ground black pepper			
Baguette, thickly sliced	½	½	½
Strong cheese, grated	225 g	8 oz	8 oz

① Preheat the slo-cooker on High.

② Heat the butter or margarine in a frying pan (skillet) and fry (sauté) the onions gently until golden brown.

③ Stir in the stock, add the bay leaf and season with salt and pepper. Bring to the boil, then transfer to the slo-cooker.

④ Cook on Low for 6–8 hours. Discard the bay leaf.

⑤ If you want a smooth consistency, purée the soup, then reheat to serve.

⑥ Sprinkle the baguette slices with the cheese and grill (broil) under a hot grill (broiler) until melted. Serve the soup in warmed bowls and float the bread and cheese slices on top.

CREAM OF ONION SOUP

—— SERVES 6 ——

Prepare as for French Onion Soup, but after puréeing stir in 150 ml/¼ pt/⅔ cup of double (heavy) cream to the puréed mixture and reheat without allowing the soup to boil.

—————— COOKING TIME: **LOW 6–8 HOURS** ——————

LENTIL SOUP
—— SERVES 6 ——

✕ ❄

	METRIC	IMPERIAL	AMERICAN
Butter or margarine	25 g	I oz	2 tbsp
Bacon rashers (slices), rinded and chopped	4	4	4
Onions, chopped	2	2	2
Carrots, chopped	2	2	2
Celery sticks, chopped	2	2	2
Water	1.2 litres	2 pts	5 cups
Tomato purée (paste)	15 ml	I tbsp	I tbsp
Bouquet garni sachet	I	I	I
Lentils	225 g	8 oz	1⅓ cups

①   Preheat the slo-cooker on High.

②   Heat the butter or margarine in a frying pan (skillet) and fry (sauté) the bacon, onions, carrots and celery gently for 3–4 minutes.

③   Add the remaining ingredients and bring to the boil, then transfer to the slo-cooker.

④   Cook on Low for 6–8 hours. Discard the bouquet garni.

⑤   Purée the soup or rub through a sieve (strainer), then reheat to serve.

TOMATO SOUP

—— SERVES 6–8 ——

✗ ❆	METRIC	IMPERIAL	AMERICAN
Butter or margarine	25 g	I oz	2 tbsp
Onion, finely chopped	I	I	I
Carrot, finely chopped	I	I	I
Celery sticks, finely chopped	2	2	2
Streaky bacon rashers (slices), rinded and chopped	4	4	4
Tomatoes, skinned	700 g	I½ lb	I½ lb
Chicken stock	900 ml	I½ pts	3¾ cups
Caster (superfine) sugar	5 ml	I tsp	I tsp
A large pinch of dried mixed herbs			
Salt and freshly ground black pepper			

① Preheat the slo-cooker on High.

② Heat the butter or margarine in a frying pan (skillet) and fry (sauté) the onion, carrot, celery and bacon gently for 3–4 minutes.

③ Stir in the remaining ingredients and bring to the boil, then transfer to the slo-cooker.

④ Cook on Low for 8–10 hours.

⑤ Stir well before serving. Alternatively, purée the soup for a smooth consistency.

CREAM OF TOMATO SOUP

—— SERVES 6–8 ——

Prepare as for Tomato Soup, but after puréeing stir in 150 ml/¼ pt/⅔ cup of double (heavy) cream and reheat without allowing the soup to boil.

FRESH WATERCRESS SOUP

—— SERVES 4–6 ——

✕ ❄

	METRIC	IMPERIAL	AMERICAN
Butter or margarine	50 g	2 oz	¼ cup
Onion, finely chopped	I	I	I
Garlic clove, crushed	I	I	I
Bunches of watercress	2	2	2
Chicken stock	600 ml	I pt	2½ cups
Salt and freshly ground black pepper			
Milk	300 ml	½ pt	I ¼ cups

1. Preheat the slo-cooker on High.
2. Heat the butter or margarine in a frying pan (skillet) and fry (sauté) the onion and garlic until transparent.
3. Reserve a few small watercress sprigs for garnish, then stir in the remainder and cook for a further 2–3 minutes, stirring all the time.
4. Add the stock and seasoning and bring to the boil, then transfer to the slo-cooker.
5. Cook on Low for 6–8 hours.
6. Purée the soup, then stir in the milk and reheat.

Freezing tip: Make and purée the soup without adding the milk, then cool and freeze the soup in a rigid container. Stir in the milk when reheating.

—— COOKING TIME: **LOW 6–8 HOURS** ——

SPINACH AND CELERY SOUP

—— SERVES 6 ——

✖ ❄

	METRIC	IMPERIAL	AMERICAN
Butter or margarine	25 g	1 oz	2 tbsp
Small head of celery, chopped	1	1	1
Onion, chopped	1	1	1
Spinach, roughly chopped	450 g	1 lb	1 lb
Water	900 ml	1½ pts	3¾ cups
Salt and freshly ground black pepper			
Milk	150 ml	¼ pt	⅔ cup
Double (heavy) cream	90 ml	6 tbsp	6 tbsp

① Preheat the slo-cooker on High.

② Heat the butter or margarine in a large frying pan (skillet) and fry (sauté) the celery and onion gently for a few minutes.

③ Add the spinach, water and salt and pepper and bring to the boil. Boil just until the spinach begins to wilt slightly, then transfer to the slo-cooker.

④ Cook on Low for 6–10 hours.

⑤ Purée the soup, stir in the milk and reheat. Swirl 15 ml/ 1 tbsp of cream in each bowl and serve.

Freezing tip: Make and purée the soup without adding the milk, then cool and freeze the soup in a rigid container. Stir in the milk when reheating.

WINTER VEGETABLE SOUP
—— SERVES 6 ——

✗ ❄

	METRIC	IMPERIAL	AMERICAN
Butter or margarine	50 g	2 oz	¼ cup
Onions, chopped	2	2	2
Carrots, diced	225 g	8 oz	8 oz
Parsnips, diced	225 g	8 oz	8 oz
Celery sticks, chopped	2	2	2
Tomatoes, skinned and chopped	225 g	8 oz	8 oz
Plain (all-purpose) flour	30 ml	2 tbsp	2 tbsp
Vegetable stock	I litre	1¾ pts	3¾ cups
Bouquet garni sachet	I	I	I
Salt and freshly ground black pepper			

① Preheat the slo-cooker on High.

② Heat the butter or margarine in a frying pan (skillet) and fry (sauté) the onions, carrots, parsnips and celery gently for about 5 minutes.

③ Stir in the tomatoes.

④ Mix the flour with a little cold stock to form a smooth paste, then stir this into the pan with the remaining stock and the bouquet garni and mix well. Season with salt and pepper. Bring to the boil, then transfer to the slo-cooker.

⑤ Cook on Low for 6–10 hours. Discard the bouquet garni.

Tip: Serve with baked potatoes sprinkled with grated cheese to make a filling meal.

—— COOKING TIME: **LOW 6–10 HOURS** ——

CREAMED SEAFOOD SOUP WITH PRAWNS

—— SERVES 4–6 ——

✖ ❄

	METRIC	IMPERIAL	AMERICAN
Streaky bacon rashers (slices), rinded and chopped	3	3	3
Onion, sliced	1	1	1
Potatoes, diced	2	2	2
Cod fillets, cut into chunks	700 g	1½ lb	1½ lb
Fish stock	300 ml	½ pt	1¼ cups
Salt and freshly ground black pepper			
Milk	150 ml	¼ pt	⅔ cup
Cooked peeled prawns (shrimp)	50 g	2 oz	2 oz

① Preheat the slo-cooker on High.

② Fry (sauté) the bacon and onion in a frying pan (skillet) until soft and transparent.

③ Add the potatoes and fry for a further 5 minutes, then transfer to the slo-cooker, add the fish and stock and season with salt and pepper.

④ Cook on High for 3–4 hours.

⑤ Stir in the milk and prawns and cook on Low for a further 1 hour.

Freezing tip: Make and purée the soup without adding the milk or prawns, then cool and freeze the soup in a rigid container. Stir in the milk and prawns when reheating.

COOKING TIME: **HIGH 3–4 HOURS, THEN LOW 1 HOUR**

CREAM OF CHICKEN SOUP
—— SERVES 4–6 ——

✗ ❄	METRIC	IMPERIAL	AMERICAN
Oil	15 ml	I tbsp	I tbsp
Chicken, diced	225 g	8 oz	8 oz
Onion, chopped	I	I	I
Pearl barley	25 g	I oz	I oz
Chopped tarragon	5 ml	I tsp	I tsp
Chicken stock	I litre	I¾ pts	4¼ cups
Salt and freshly ground black pepper			
Double (heavy) cream	300 ml	½ pt	I¼ cups

① Preheat the slo-cooker on High.

② Heat the oil in a frying pan (skillet) and fry (sauté) the chicken and onion until soft. Transfer to the slo-cooker and add all the remaining ingredients except the cream.

③ Cook on Low for 6–10 hours.

④ Purée the soup, then stir in the cream and reheat gently without allowing the soup to boil.

Freezing tip: Make and purée the soup without adding the cream, then cool and freeze the soup in a rigid container. Stir in the cream when reheating.

CURRIED APPLE SOUP

—— SERVES 6 ——

✗ ❄	METRIC	IMPERIAL	AMERICAN
Butter or margarine	25 g	1 oz	2 tbsp
Onion, finely chopped	1	1	1
Curry powder	10–15 ml	2–3 tsp	2–3 tsp
Plain (all-purpose) flour	30 ml	2 tbsp	2 tbsp
Chicken stock	1 litre	1¾ pts	4¼ cups
Grated rind and juice of ½ lemon			
Cooking (tart) apples, peeled, cored and chopped	700 g	1½ lb	1½ lb
Salt and freshly ground black pepper			
Soured (dairy sour) cream or plain yoghurt	150 ml	¼ pt	⅔ cup

① Preheat the slo-cooker on High.

② Heat the butter or margarine in a frying pan (skillet) and fry (sauté) the onion until transparent.

③ Stir in the curry powder and flour, then gradually add the stock, lemon rind and juice and apples. Season well with salt and pepper. Bring to the boil, then transfer to the slo-cooker.

④ Cook on Low for 6–8 hours.

⑤ Purée the soup, then reheat and stir in the cream or yoghurt.

Freezing tip: Make and purée the soup without adding the cream or yoghurt, then cool and freeze the soup in a rigid container. Stir in the cream or yoghurt when reheating.

CHILLED CUCUMBER AND MINT SOUP
—— SERVES 6 ——

✂ ❄

	METRIC	IMPERIAL	AMERICAN
Butter or margarine	25 g	I cz	2 tbsp
Onion, chopped	I	I	I
Large cucumber, peeled and sliced	I	I	I
Chicken or vegetable stock	600 ml	I pt	2½ cups
Chopped mint leaves	30 ml	2 tbsp	2 tbsp
Salt and freshly ground black pepper			
Milk	300 ml	½ pt	1¼ cups
Plain yoghurt or crème fraîche	90 ml	6 tbsp	6 tbsp

① Preheat the slo-cooker on High.

② Heat the butter or margarine in a frying pan (skillet) and fry (sauté) the onion until transparent.

③ Stir in the cucumber, stock, mint and salt and pepper and bring to the boil. Transfer to the slo-cooker

④ Cook on Low for 4–8 hours.

⑤ Purée the soup and stir in the milk.

⑥ Allow to cool, then chill until ready to serve in chilled bowls with 15 ml/1 tbsp yoghurt or crème fraîche in each bowl.

Freezing tip: Make and purée the soup without adding the milk, then cool and freeze the soup in a rigid container. Stir in the milk when reheating.

Tip: This soup can also be served hot with crisp bread croûtons.

VICHYSSOISE
—— SERVES 6 ——

✕ ❄	METRIC	IMPERIAL	AMERICAN
Unsalted (sweet) butter	50 g	2 oz	¼ cup
Onions, chopped	2	2	2
Garlic clove, crushed	I	I	I
Leeks, thinly sliced	700 g	1½ lb	1½ lb
Potatoes, chopped	2	2	2
Chicken stock	900 ml	1½ pts	3¾ cups
Salt and freshly ground black pepper			
Double (heavy) cream	90 ml	6 tbsp	6 tbsp
Snipped fresh chives			

① Preheat the slo-cooker on High.

② Heat the butter in a frying pan (skillet) and fry (sauté) the onions, garlic and leeks gently for 3–4 minutes.

③ Add the potatoes and stock, season with salt and pepper and bring to the boil, then transfer to the slo-cooker.

④ Cook on Low for 8–10 hours.

⑤ Purée the soup or rub through a sieve (strainer).

⑥ Allow to cool, then chill until ready to serve garnished with a swirl of cream and sprinkled with chives.

Freezing tip: Make the soup without adding the garlic, then cool and freeze the soup in a rigid container. Season with crushed garlic or garlic salt when ready to serve and garnish with the cream and chives.

MULLIGATAWNY SOUP

—— SERVES 4–6 ——

✗ ❄

	METRIC	IMPERIAL	AMERICAN
Butter or margarine	50 g	2 oz	¼ cup
Cooking (tart) apple, peeled and sliced	I	I	I
Onion, sliced	I	I	I
Carrot, sliced	I	I	I
Curry powder	30 ml	2 tbsp	2 tbsp
Plain (all-purpose) flour	45 ml	3 tbsp	3 tbsp
Chicken or vegetable stock	I litre	1¾ pts	4¼ cups
Chicken portions, skinned	2	2	2
A few drops of lemon juice			
Salt and freshly ground black pepper			

① Preheat the slo-cooker on High.

② Heat the butter or margarine in a frying pan (skillet) and fry (sauté) the apple, onion and carrot for 2–3 minutes.

③ Stir in the curry powder and flour and fry for 1 minute.

④ Stir in the stock and bring to the boil, then transfer to the slo-cooker.

⑤ Add the chicken portions and cook on High for 4–5 hours.

⑥ Remove the chicken portions and slice the meat.

⑦ Purée the vegetables and stock, then return the chicken. Season with lemon juice, salt and pepper and serve.

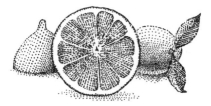

—— COOKING TIME: **HIGH 4–5 HOURS** ——

EGGS FLORENTINE
—— SERVES 4 ——

✂ ①

	METRIC	IMPERIAL	AMERICAN
Butter or margarine	25 g	I oz	2 tbsp
Spinach, roughly chopped	450 g	I lb	I lb
Eggs	4	4	4
For the white sauce:			
Butter or margarine	25 g	I oz	2 tbsp
Plain (all-purpose) flour	25 g	I oz	¼ cup
Milk	300 ml	½ pt	I ¼ cups
Salt and freshly ground black pepper			
Cheese, finely grated	75 g	3 oz	¾ cup

① Butter the inside of the slo-cooker and preheat on High.

② Arrange the spinach in the slo-cooker and cook on High for 1 hour.

③ To make the white sauce, heat the butter or margarine in a pan and stir in the flour. Cook gently for 2–3 minutes, stirring continuously.

④ Gradually add the milk, still stirring, and bring to the boil. Season well with salt and pepper.

⑤ Use the base of a cup to make four 'wells' in the spinach. Break one egg into each, then pour over the prepared sauce.

⑥ Cook on High for a further 2 hours.

⑦ Serve sprinkled with the grated cheese.

—— COOKING TIME: **HIGH 3 HOURS** ——

AVOCADO WITH CRAB

—— SERVES 4–6 ——

	METRIC	IMPERIAL	AMERICAN
Avocados	2	2	2
Salt			
Lemon juice			
Butter or margarine	15 g	½ oz	I tbsp
Plain (all-purpose) flour	15 ml	I tbsp	I tbsp
Milk	150 ml	¼ pt	⅔ cup
Tomatoes, skinned, quartered and sliced	3	3	3
Tomato purée (paste)	30 ml	2 tbsp	2 tbsp
Can of crab meat, drained	100 g	4 oz	I small
A pinch of grated nutmeg			
Water	150 ml	¼ pt	⅔ cup
Green salad, to garnish			

① Preheat the slo-cooker on High.

② Halve and stone (pit) the avocados and sprinkle with salt and lemon juice to prevent discoloration.

③ Melt the butter or margarine, stir in the flour and cook for 1 minute, stirring. Whisk in the milk, then bring to the boil, stirring continuously, and cook until thickened.

④ Stir in the tomatoes, tomato purée, crab meat and nutmeg.

⑤ Spoon the crab mixture into the hollows of the avocado halves and arrange in the slo-cooker. Pour the water around them.

⑥ Cook on Low for 2–3 hours.

⑦ Serve with a green salad garnish.

CHICKEN LIVER PÂTÉ
—— SERVES 8–10 ——

✗ ❄

	METRIC	IMPERIAL	AMERICAN
Streaky bacon rashers (slices), rinded	4	4	4
Chicken livers	450 g	1 lb	1 lb
Onion, sliced	1	1	1
Whole cloves	2	2	2
Bay leaves	2	2	2
Bouquet garni sachet	1	1	1
Salt and freshly ground black pepper			
Butter or margarine	50 g	2 oz	¼ cup
Plain (all-purpose) flour	50 g	2 oz	½ cup
Milk	150 ml	¼ pt	⅔ cup
Garlic clove, crushed	1	1	1
Double (heavy) cream	30 ml	2 tbsp	2 tbsp
Egg	1	1	1
Melba toast or crusty bread, to serve			

① Preheat the slo-cooker on High.

② Stretch the bacon slices with the back of a knife, then lay them across the base of an ovenproof pâté dish.

③ Put the livers, onion, cloves, bay leaves, bouquet garni and a pinch of salt in a pan and just cover with water. Bring to the boil, then simmer for a few minutes until the livers stiffen. Leave to cool.

④ Discard the cloves, bay leaves and bouquet garni. Put the liver, onions and 30 ml/2 tbsp of the water into a food processor and purée until smooth.

⑤ Heat the butter or margarine in a pan, stir in the flour and cook for 1 minute. Gradually stir in the milk, then bring to the boil and simmer for 2 minutes, stirring continuously. Add the liver, garlic, cream and egg and season with salt and pepper. Transfer to the prepared dish, cover with foil and place in the slo-cooker. Surround with sufficient boiling water to come almost to the top of the dish.

⑥ Cook on High for 5–7 hours.

⑦ Allow to cool, then chill before serving with melba toast or crusty bread.

Freezing tip: Pâté is best frozen in slices interleaved with greaseproof (waxed) paper.

CHICKEN AND LAMB PÂTÉ
—— SERVES 6 ——

✂ ❄

	METRIC	IMPERIAL	AMERICAN
Butter or margarine	25 g	1 oz	2 tbsp
Streaky bacon rashers (slices), rinded	4	4	4
Onion, finely chopped	1	1	1
Chicken livers	225 g	8 oz	8 oz
Lambs' liver	225 g	8 oz	8 oz
Belly pork, minced (ground)	225 g	8 oz	8 oz
Garlic clove, crushed	1	1	1
Egg, beaten	1	1	1
Double (heavy) cream	30 ml	2 tbsp	2 tbsp
Mustard powder	5 ml	1 tsp	1 tsp
Dried sage	5 ml	1 tsp	1 tsp
Salt and freshly ground black pepper			
Crusty bread, to serve			

① Preheat the slo-cooker on High.

② Grease a 15 cm/6 in cake tin (pan) with a little of the butter or margarine. Stretch the bacon rashers by running them over the blunt edge of a knife, then line the prepared tin with the bacon, leaving the edges hanging over the sides.

③ Melt the remaining butter or margarine in a frying pan (skillet) and fry (sauté) the onion until transparent.

④ Add the chicken and lambs' livers and fry for 1 minute until sealed.

⑤ Mince (grind) the mixture, then mix with the remaining ingredients and spoon into the prepared container. Press down lightly, fold the ends of the bacon over the top and cover with foil.

⑥ Place in the slo-cooker and surround with sufficient boiling water to come half-way up the tin. Cook on High for 3–4 hours.

⑦ Remove the tin from the slo-cooker and place a weight on the top while the pâté cools

⑧ Serve with crusty bread.

Freezing tip: Pâté is best frozen in slices interleaved with greaseproof (waxed) paper.

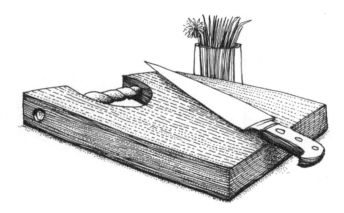

SEAFOOD

Fish and seafood cooked in the slo-cooker retain every bit of delicate flavour and also remain beautifully whole. The moist heat is so gentle that whole fish or fish pieces do not disintegrate.

Slo-cooking takes away the exact timing normally necessary for fish cookery, although it does cook more quickly than, say, meat or soup.

Because fish should be appreciated at its freshest, I think it should be eaten as soon as it is cooked, so I do not think it is a good idea to freeze any of these recipes. Always thaw frozen fish completely before using in any of these recipes.

SEAFOOD TIPS

◇ Clean and trim fish in the usual way before cooking.

◇ Do not put too many whole fish in a slo-cooker or the weight of the top ones could affect the finished appearance and texture of those at the bottom. Four is an ideal number.

◇ You can use stock, water, wine, cider or fruit juice to cook fish. You will need only small quantities to retain the most fish flavour.

◇ Thickening agents such as flour or cornflour (cornstarch) should be added to casserole-type dishes before slo-cooking (see page 11). Where there is a sauce made from the cooking liquor to accompany the fish, you may prefer to thicken the sauce in a pan after cooking, while keeping the cooked fish warm.

◇ Cream, milk and egg yolks should be added to the slo-cooker during the last 30 minutes of cooking.

◇ When adapting your own fish recipes, compare them with the recipes in this chapter. You will probably need less liquid in which to cook the dishes.

TOMATO-BAKED MACKEREL AND COD
—— SERVES 4 ——

✕	METRIC	IMPERIAL	AMERICAN
Butter or margarine	25 g	1 oz	2 tbsp
Onion, finely chopped	1	1	1
Mackerel fillets, skinned and cubed	450 g	1 lb	1 lb
Cod fillets, skinned and cubed	450 g	1 lb	1 lb
Button mushrooms, sliced	100 g	4 oz	4 oz
Tomatoes, skinned and sliced	225 g	8 oz	8 oz
Juice of lemon	1	1	1
Water	45 ml	3 tbsp	3 tbsp
Salt and freshly ground black pepper			
Fried (sautéed) bread triangles, to garnish			

① Preheat the slo-cooker on High.

② Heat the butter or margarine in a frying pan (skillet) and fry the onion gently until transparent.

③ Stir in the remaining ingredients and bring to the boil, then transfer to the slo-cooker.

④ Cook on Low for 2–4 hours.

⑤ Serve garnished with triangles of fried bread.

—————— COOKING TIME: **LOW 2–4 HOURS** ——————

HADDOCK CASSEROLE WITH COURGETTES
——SERVES 4——

✂	METRIC	IMPERIAL	AMERICAN
Haddock or other white fish, skinned and cubed	700 g	1½ lb	1½ lb
Cornflour (cornstarch)	15 ml	1 tbsp	1 tbsp
Oil	15 ml	1 tbsp	1 tbsp
Onion, finely chopped	1	1	1
Garlic clove, crushed	1	1	1
Courgettes (zucchini), thinly sliced	225 g	8 oz	8 oz
Dry white wine or cider	300 ml	½ pt	1¼ cups
Bay leaf	1	1	1
Bouquet garni sachet	1	1	1

① Preheat the slo-cooker on High.

② Toss the fish with the cornflour until it is well covered, shaking off any excess.

③ Heat the oil in a frying pan (skillet) and fry (sauté) the onion, garlic and courgettes gently for 4–5 minutes.

④ Add the wine or cider, bay leaf and bouquet garni, then stir in the fish. Bring to the boil, then transfer to the slo-cooker.

⑤ Cook on Low for 3–6 hours.

⑥ Discard the bay leaf and bouquet garni before serving.

SMOKED HADDOCK WITH EGGS

—— SERVES 4 ——

✗	METRIC	IMPERIAL	AMERICAN
Butter or margarine	25 g	1 oz	2 tbsp
Smoked haddock, in four equal pieces	700 g	1½ lb	1½ lb
Milk	90 ml	6 tbsp	6 tbsp
Water	90 ml	6 tbsp	6 tbsp
Freshly ground black pepper			
Eggs	4	4	4

①   Butter the inside of the slo-cooker and preheat on High.

②   Arrange the haddock pieces in the slo-cooker and pour over enough of the milk and water just to cover. Season with pepper.

③   Cook on Low for 2 hours.

④   Crack the eggs over the fish and continue to cook on Low for a further 1 hour.

⑤   Serve immediately.

HERRING WITH GOOSEBERRIES
—— SERVES 4–6 ——

✖	METRIC	IMPERIAL	AMERICAN
Butter or margarine	15 g	½ oz	1 tbsp
Boned herrings	450 g	1 lb	1 lb
Salt and freshly ground black pepper			
Gooseberries, trimmed	225 g	8 oz	8 oz
Caster (superfine) sugar	30 ml	2 tbsp	2 tbsp
Water	75 ml	5 tbsp	5 tbsp

① Butter the base of the slo-cooker and preheat on High.

② Season the inside of the herrings with salt and pepper.

③ Arrange the gooseberries in the slo-cooker, sprinkle with the sugar and pour on the water. Lay the seasoned herrings on top.

④ Cook on Low for 2–3 hours.

ROLLMOP HERRINGS
—— SERVES 4 ——

✂	METRIC	IMPERIAL	AMERICAN
Herrings	6–8	6–8	6–8
Salt and freshly ground black pepper			
Malt vinegar	150 ml	¼ pt	⅔ cup
Water	150 ml	¼ pt	⅔ cup
Shallots, thinly sliced	3	3	3
Bay leaves	2	2	2
Blade of mace	1	1	1
Black peppercorns	6	6	6
Salad and boiled potatoes, to serve (optional)			

① Preheat the slo-cooker on High.

② Scale, clean and bone the herrings and discard the heads and tails. Season lightly with salt and pepper. Roll up from the tail end, skin-side out, and arrange in the slo-cooker.

③ Mix together the remaining ingredients in a saucepan and season with salt and pepper. Bring to the boil, then pour over the herrings.

④ Cook on Low for 4–6 hours.

⑤ Arrange the herrings in a serving dish and pour over the cooking liquor. Serve hot with salad and boiled potatoes if wished, or leave to cool and serve as a starter.

Variation: Small, boned mackerel or pilchards can be cooked in the same way.

STUFFED PLAICE WITH ORANGE

—— SERVES 4 ——

✗	METRIC	IMPERIAL	AMERICAN
Butter or margarine	50 g	2 oz	¼ cup
Mushrooms, chopped	100 g	4 oz	4 oz
Hard-boiled (hard-cooked) eggs, chopped	2	2	2
Salt and freshly ground black pepper			
Small plaice fillets, skinned	8	8	8
Juice of oranges	2	2	2

① Preheat the slo-cooker on High.

② Heat 15 g/½ oz/1 tbsp of the butter or margarine in a saucepan and gently fry (sauté) the mushrooms for 1–2 minutes.

③ Stir in the eggs and season with salt and pepper.

④ Place a little of the mixture on the skinned side of each fillet. Roll up and secure with cocktail sticks (toothpicks).

⑤ Arrange the fish in the slo-cooker and dot with the remaining butter or margarine. Pour over the orange juice.

⑥ Cook on Low for 2½–3 hours.

—— COOKING TIME: **LOW 2½–3 HOURS**——

ITALIAN-STYLE MULLET

—— SERVES 4 ——

✕	METRIC	IMPERIAL	AMERICAN
Butter or margarine	25 g	1 oz	2 tbsp
Tomatoes, skinned and sliced	2	2	2
Green (bell) pepper, seeded and sliced	1	1	1
Mushrooms, sliced	100 g	4 oz	4 oz
Salt and freshly ground black pepper			
Medium red mullet	4	4	4
Red wine	60 ml	4 tbsp	4 tbsp
Snipped chives	15 ml	1 tbsp	1 tbsp

① Grease the slo-cooker with a little of the butter or margarine and preheat on High.

② Arrange the tomato, pepper and mushroom slices in the slo-cooker and season with salt and pepper.

③ Scale and trim the fish, then place on top of the vegetables and season with salt and pepper. Pour over the wine and dot with the remaining butter or margarine. Sprinkle with the chives.

④ Cook on High for 2–3 hours.

CREAMY FISH PIE
—— SERVES 4 ——

✕	METRIC	IMPERIAL	AMERICAN
Cod or haddock fillets, skinned and diced	450 g	1 lb	1 lb
Onion, chopped	1	1	1
Garlic clove, crushed	1	1	1
Button mushrooms, sliced	100 g	4 oz	4 oz
Parsley sprigs	3	3	3
Bay leaf	1	1	1
Salt and freshly ground black pepper			
Fish or vegetable stock	150 ml	¼ pt	⅔ cup
Butter or margarine	25 g	1 oz	2 tbsp
Plain (all-purpose) flour	30 ml	2 tbsp	2 tbsp
Milk	250 ml	8 fl oz	1 cup
Hard-boiled (hard-cooked) egg, sliced	1	1	1
Chopped parsley	15 ml	1 tbsp	1 tbsp
Potatoes, cooked and mashed	700 g	1½ lb	1½ lb

① Preheat the slo-cooker on High.

② Arrange the fish, onion, garlic and mushrooms in the slo-cooker. Add the parsley sprigs and bay leaf and season with salt and pepper. Pour over the stock and stir gently.

③ Cook on High for 2–3 hours.

④ Strain the liquid and reserve 150 ml/¼ pt/⅔ cup.

⑤ Melt the butter or margarine in a saucepan, stir in the flour and cook gently for 1 minute. Whisk in the milk and the reserved liquid, then bring to the boil and simmer for 2 minutes, stirring. Season with salt and pepper.

⑥ Pour the sauce over the fish, add the eggs and stir gently.

⑦ Mix the chopped parsley into the cooked potatoes and spread over the top of the dish. Brown in a preheated oven at 200°C/400°F/gas mark 6 or under a hot grill (broiler).

———— COOKING TIME: **HIGH 2–3 HOURS** ————

PRAWN RISOTTO

—— SERVES 4 ——

✕ ①

	METRIC	IMPERIAL	AMERICAN
Oil	15 ml	I tbsp	I tbsp
Onions, finely chopped	2	2	2
Chicken stock	900 ml	1½ pts	3¾ cups
Button mushrooms, sliced	225 g	8 oz	8 oz
Green (bell) pepper, seeded and chopped	I	I	I
Tomatoes, skinned and sliced	2	2	2
Easy-cook long-grain rice	175 g	6 oz	¾ cup
Peeled prawns (shrimp)	225 g	8 oz	8 oz
Salt and freshly ground black pepper			

① Preheat the slo-cooker on High.

② Heat the oil in a frying pan (skillet) and fry (sauté) the onions gently until transparent.

③ Add the stock, mushrooms and pepper and bring to the boil, then transfer to the slo-cooker.

④ Stir in the tomatoes, rice and prawns.

⑤ Cook on Low for 3–4 hours.

⑥ Stir well, taste and adjust the seasoning, then serve at once.

——— COOKING TIME: **LOW 3–4 HOURS** ———

MEAT

The slo-cooker could almost have been designed specifically for cooking meat, both joints and casseroles. The recipes can be left to cook all day (and part of the evening too, if necessary) with no risk of burning or overcooking, and without the worry of checking, basting, turning or stirring. The slow, gentle heat action tenderises even the toughest cuts of meat and cooked joints will shrink much less than when cooked conventionally.

Use the slo-cooker to prepare exotic, delicate recipes suitable for entertaining as well as for tasty casseroles, stews and roasts for every day. Whenever possible, use the juices that surround the meat as a rich sauce to complete the meal.

The majority of slo-cooked meat recipes can be frozen successfully. Any specific tips you need can be found at the end of the recipes. Always defrost frozen meat completely before slo-cooking. Remember, though, that partially frozen meat is easy to handle when chopping or slicing.

MEAT TIPS

◇ Trim excess fat from the meat before cooking.

◇ Lightly browning the meat before slo-cooking improves the flavour and appearance of joints and casseroles.

◇ Vegetables take longer to cook than meat so make sure they are diced small and immersed in the cooking liquid.

◇ Reduce the quantity of liquid by about half if you are adapting your own conventional recipes. If necessary, you can adjust the quantity of liquid before serving.

◇ Liquids for slo-cooking meat can be water, stock, wine, cider, beer or fruit juice.

◇ If you are thickening a casserole, do so before cooking or for the final 1–1½ hours (see page 11), or thicken the cooking juices separately in a pan after you have cooked the meat.

◇ Add cream, milk or egg yolks during the final 30 minutes of cooking.

◇ Cooking times for joints vary according to size, shape, quality, the proportion of meat to fat and bone, and personal taste. However, these guidelines should be helpful: cook a 1.25–1.5 kg (2½–3 lb) joint on High for 3–6 hours (3–5 hours for pork); cook a 1.6–2.25 kg (3½–5 lb) joint on High for 5–8 hours (4–6 hours for pork).

◇ To obtain a crisp skin for pork, do not fry (sauté) the joint before slo-cooking. Instead, finish the cooked joint under a hot grill (broiler) for about 10 minutes.

BEEF GOULASH
—— SERVES 6 ——

✗ ❋

	METRIC	IMPERIAL	AMERICAN
Plain (all-purpose) flour	45 ml	3 tbsp	3 tbsp
Salt and freshly ground black pepper			
Stewing steak, cubed	I kg	2¼ lb	2¼ lb
Oil	45 ml	3 tbsp	3 tbsp
Onions, chopped	3	3	3
Green (bell) peppers, seeded and sliced	2	2	2
Beef stock	300 ml	½ pt	1¼ cups
Can of tomatoes	400 g	14 oz	I large
Tomato purée (paste)	45 ml	3 tbsp	3 tbsp
Paprika	15 ml	I tbsp	I tbsp
Bouquet garni sachet	I	I	I
Soured (dairy sour) cream or plain yoghurt, to garnish			

①   Preheat the slo-cooker on High.

②   Season the flour with salt and pepper, then toss the meat in the flour, shaking off any excess.

③   Heat the oil in a frying pan (skillet) and brown the meat lightly on all sides.

④   Stir in the onions and peppers and cook for 3 minutes.

⑤   Stir in the remaining ingredients and bring to the boil, then transfer to the slo-cooker.

⑥   Cook on Low for 7–10 hours.

⑦   Discard the bouquet garni, adjust the seasoning to taste and stir well. Serve with a swirl of soured cream or yoghurt.

Freezing tip: Freeze without the cream or yoghurt.

BEEF IN RED WINE

—— SERVES 6 ——

✗ ✱	METRIC	IMPERIAL	AMERICAN
Oil	15 ml	1 tbsp	1 tbsp
Butter	25 g	1 oz	2 tbsp
Streaky bacon, rinded and chopped	225 g	8 oz	8 oz
Garlic cloves, crushed	2	2	2
Stewing steak, cubed	1 kg	2¼ lb	2¼ lb
Plain (all-purpose) flour	30 ml	2 tbsp	2 tbsp
Red wine	300 ml	½ pt	1¼ cups
Bay leaves	2	2	2
Whole small onions	12	12	12
Salt and freshly ground black pepper			

① Preheat the slo-cooker on High.

② Heat the oil and butter in a frying pan (skillet) and fry (sauté) the bacon and garlic gently for 2–3 minutes.

③ Add the steak and stir over a low heat until lightly browned on all sides.

④ Stir in the flour, then slowly add the red wine, stirring until well blended. Add the bay leaves, onions and seasoning. Bring to the boil, then transfer to the slo-cooker.

⑤ Cook on Low for 7–10 hours.

⑥ Discard the bay leaves and adjust the seasoning to taste before serving.

Freezing tip: Cook without the garlic. Add crushed garlic or garlic salt when reheating.

BEEF STROGANOFF

— SERVES 4 —

	METRIC	IMPERIAL	AMERICAN
Butter or margarine	50 g	2 oz	¼ cup
Onions, chopped	2	2	2
Plain (all-purpose) flour	30 ml	2 tbsp	2 tbsp
Salt and freshly ground black pepper			
Braising steak, cut into strips across the grain	700 g	1½ lb	1½ lb
Beef stock	300 ml	½ pt	1¼ cups
Mushrooms, sliced	100 g	4 oz	4 oz
Dried mixed herbs	5 ml	1 tsp	1 tsp
Tomato purée (paste)	15 ml	1 tbsp	1 tbsp
French mustard	10 ml	2 tsp	2 tsp
Single (light) cream	150 ml	¼ pt	⅔ cup
Chopped parsley	15 ml	1 tbsp	1 tbsp

① Preheat the slo-cooker on High.

② Heat the butter or margarine in a large frying pan (skillet) and gently fry (sauté) the onions until transparent.

③ Season the flour with salt and pepper, then toss the meat in the flour, shaking off any excess.

④ Add the meat to the onions and stir until browned.

⑤ Stir in all the remaining ingredients except the cream and parsley and bring to the boil, then transfer to the slo-cooker.

⑥ Cook on Low for 7–10 hours.

⑦ Just before serving, stir well, swirl the cream on top and garnish with the parsley.

Freezing tip: Omit the cream and parsley before freezing. Stir the cream into the dish after reheating but do not allow the mixture to boil.

COOKING TIME: **LOW 7–10 HOURS**

BEEF OLIVES

—— SERVES 4 ——

⚠ ❄

	METRIC	IMPERIAL	AMERICAN
Braising steak	450 g	I lb	I lb
Oil	30 ml	2 tbsp	2 tbsp
Onion, sliced	I	I	I
Plain (all-purpose) flour	30 ml	2 tbsp	2 tbsp
Beef stock	450 ml	¾ pt	2 cups
For the stuffing:			
Fresh breadcrumbs	50 g	2 oz	I cup
Shredded suet	25 g	I oz	2 tbsp
Dried mixed herbs	2.5 ml	½ tsp	½ tsp
Chopped parsley	5 ml	I tsp	I tsp
Salt and freshly ground black pepper			
Egg, beaten	I	I	I
Lemon juice	5 ml	I tsp	I tsp

① Preheat the slo-cooker on High.

② Cut the steak into about eight thin slices across the grain, each about 10 cm/4 in square.

③ Mix the stuffing ingredients and spread a little on to each slice. Roll up and secure with cocktail sticks (toothpicks).

④ Heat the oil in a frying pan (skillet) and lightly brown the meat rolls. Remove from the pan.

⑤ In the same pan, fry (sauté) the onion until transparent. Stir in the flour and cook until browned. Gradually stir in the stock and season to taste with salt and pepper. Bring to the boil, stirring well, then transfer to the slo-cooker and arrange the meat on top.

⑥ Cook on Low for 6–9 hours.

⑦ Arrange the beef olives on a serving plate and remove the cotton or cocktail sticks. Keep warm.

⑧ Strain the gravy and reheat in a small pan if necessary. Pour over the meat just before serving.

—— COOKING TIME: **LOW 6–9 HOURS**——

SPAGHETTI BOLOGNESE

—— SERVES 4 ——

	METRIC	IMPERIAL	AMERICAN
Oil	30 ml	2 tbsp	2 tbsp
Onion, chopped	1	1	1
Carrot, chopped	1	1	1
Celery stick, chopped	1	1	1
Garlic cloves, crushed	2	2	2
Minced (ground) beef	450 g	1 lb	1 lb
Mushrooms, chopped	50 g	2 oz	2 oz
Can of chopped tomatoes	400 g	14 oz	1 large
Bay leaf	1	1	1
Dried oregano	2.5 ml	½ tsp	½ tsp
Salt and freshly ground black pepper			
Spaghetti	225 g	8 oz	8 oz

① Preheat the slo-cooker on High.

② Heat the oil in a large frying pan (skillet) and fry (sauté) the onion, carrot, celery and garlic until transparent.

③ Add the meat and fry, stirring well, until it is browned and well broken up.

④ Stir in the mushrooms, tomatoes, bay leaf and oregano and season to taste with salt and pepper. Transfer to the slo-cooker.

⑤ Cook on High for 3–4 hours.

⑥ When almost ready to serve, bring a large pan of salted water to the boil, toss in the spaghetti and boil until *al dente*. Drain well.

⑦ Remove the bay leaf from the Bolognese sauce and serve the sauce with the spaghetti.

BEEF LASAGNE

—— SERVES 4 ——

✕ ❄	METRIC	IMPERIAL	AMERICAN
Oil	30 ml	2 tbsp	2 tbsp
Onion, chopped	1	1	1
Garlic clove, chopped	1	1	1
Carrot, chopped	1	1	1
Celery stick, chopped	1	1	1
Minced (ground) beef	450 g	1 lb	1 lb
Mushrooms, chopped	50 g	2 oz	2 oz
Plain (all-purpose) flour	15 ml	1 tbsp	1 tbsp
Tomato purée (paste)	30 ml	2 tbsp	2 tbsp
Chopped flatleaf parsley	15 ml	1 tbsp	1 tbsp
Salt and freshly ground black pepper			
White Sauce (see page 34)	300 ml	½ pt	1¼ cups
No-need-to-precook lasagne sheets	175 g	6 oz	6 oz
Parmesan cheese, freshly grated	50 g	2 oz	½ cup

① Preheat the slo-cooker on High.

② Heat the oil in a large frying pan (skillet) and fry (sauté) the onion, garlic, carrot and celery until transparent.

③ Stir in the beef and fry until well browned and broken up. Stir in the mushrooms.

④ Mix in the flour and cook until browned. Stir in the tomato purée and parsley and season with salt and pepper.

⑤ Make up the white sauce.

⑥ Layer the meat, lasagne sheets and white sauce into the slo-cooker, finishing with a layer of lasagne, then white sauce. Sprinkle with half the Parmesan.

⑦ Cook on Low for 4–6 hours.

⑧ Serve sprinkled with the remaining Parmesan.

—————— COOKING TIME: **LOW 4–6 HOURS**——————

CHILLI CON CARNE

— SERVES 4 —

✂ ❄	METRIC	IMPERIAL	AMERICAN
Oil	15 ml	1 tbsp	1 tbsp
Streaky bacon, rinded and chopped	50 g	2 oz	2 oz
Onion, chopped	1	1	1
Green (bell) pepper, seeded and chopped	1	1	1
Celery sticks, chopped	2	2	2
Minced (ground) beef	450 g	1 lb	1 lb
Chilli powder	10 ml	2 tsp	2 tsp
Can of red kidney beans, drained and rinsed	400 g	14 oz	1 large
Can of chopped tomatoes	400 g	14 oz	1 large
Salt and freshly ground black pepper			
Tacos and a green salad, to serve			

① Preheat the slo-cooker on High.

② Heat the oil in a large frying pan (skillet) and fry (sauté) the bacon, onion, pepper and celery until transparent.

③ Stir in the beef and fry until lightly browned and well broken up.

④ Stir in the chilli powder, kidney beans and tomatoes and season with salt and pepper. Transfer to the slo-cooker.

⑤ Cook on Low for 6–8 hours.

⑥ Check and adjust the seasoning before serving with tacos and a green salad.

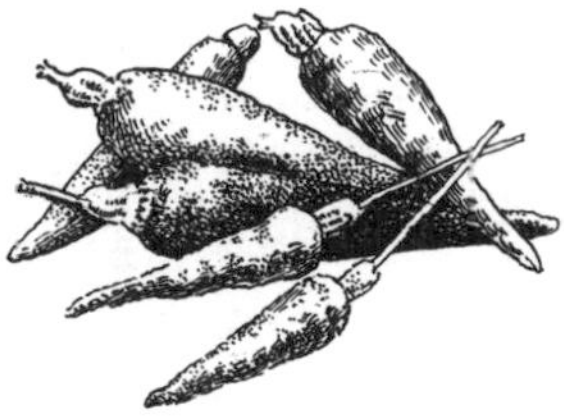

COOKING TIME: **LOW 6–8 HOURS**

BEEFBURGERS IN TOMATO SAUCE

—— SERVES 4 ——

⚠ ❄

	METRIC	IMPERIAL	AMERICAN
Minced (ground) beef	450 g	1 lb	1 lb
Fresh breadcrumbs	100 g	4 oz	2 cups
Small onion, finely chopped	1	1	1
Dried mixed herbs	10 ml	2 tsp	2 tsp
Salt and freshly ground black pepper			
Butter or margarine	25 g	1 oz	2 tbsp
Beef stock cube	1	1	1
Boiling water	150 ml	¼ pt	⅔ cup
Can of condensed cream of tomato soup	10 oz	275 g	1 medium

① Preheat the slo-cooker on High.

② Mix together the minced beef, breadcrumbs, onion, herbs and seasoning. Shape into eight beefburgers.

③ Heat the butter or margarine in a frying pan (skillet) and brown the burgers quickly on both sides. Transfer to the slo-cooker.

④ Dissolve the stock cube in the boiling water, then mix into the tomato soup. Pour into the frying pan, mix with the cooking juices from the burgers and bring to the boil. Pour the sauce over the burgers.

⑤ Cook on Low for 4–6 hours.

Freezing tip: Arrange the burgers on a foil tray and pour over the sauce. Cover and freeze.

SAUSAGE AND MUSHROOM BAKE
—— SERVES 6 ——

✂ ❄

	METRIC	IMPERIAL	AMERICAN
Oil	30 ml	2 tbsp	2 tbsp
Onion, chopped	1	1	1
Potatoes, thinly sliced	450 g	1 lb	1 lb
Skinless beef sausages, halved	450 g	1 lb	1 lb
Can of baked beans	450 g	1 lb	1 large
Button mushrooms, halved	100 g	4 oz	4 oz
Chilli powder	15 ml	1 tbsp	1 tbsp
Tomato purée (paste)	15 ml	1 tbsp	1 tbsp
Water	150 ml	¼ pt	⅔ cup
Salt and freshly ground black pepper			

①   Preheat the slo-cooker on High.

②   Heat the oil in a large frying pan (skillet) and fry (sauté) the onion and potatoes gently for 5 minutes.

③   Add the remaining ingredients, season with salt and pepper and bring to the boil. Transfer to the slo-cooker.

④   Cook on Low for 6–10 hours.

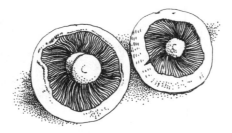

—— COOKING TIME: **LOW 6–10 HOURS** ——

LAMB CUTLETS IN RED WINE SAUCE

—— SERVES 4 ——

✗ ❋

	METRIC	IMPERIAL	AMERICAN
Oil	30 ml	2 tbsp	2 tbsp
Onions, thinly sliced into rings	2	2	2
Lamb cutlets	8	8	8
Salt and freshly ground black pepper			
Cornflour (cornstarch)	15 ml	1 tbsp	1 tbsp
Red wine	300 ml	½ pt	1¼ cups
Dried rosemary	10 ml	2 tsp	2 tsp

① Preheat the slo-cooker on High.

② Heat the oil in a frying pan (skillet) and fry (sauté) the onions gently until transparent. Transfer to the slo-cooker.

③ Season the lamb cutlets with salt and pepper, then brown on all sides in the same pan. Arrange on top of the onions in the slo-cooker.

④ Stir the cornflour into the remaining fat in the pan, then slowly add the red wine, stirring continuously. Add the rosemary. Bring to the boil, then pour the sauce over the cutlets.

⑤ Cook on Low for 4–6 hours.

—————— COOKING TIME: **LOW 4–6 HOURS**——————

LAMB IN MUSHROOM SAUCE

—— SERVES 4–6 ——

✕ ❄

	METRIC	IMPERIAL	AMERICAN
Oil	15 ml	I tbsp	I tbsp
Butter or margarine	25 g	I oz	2 tbsp
Onions, thinly sliced	2	2	2
Garlic clove, crushed	I	I	I
Green (bell) pepper, seeded and sliced	I	I	I
Lean lamb, cubed	700 g	1¾ lb	1¾ lb
Mushrooms, sliced	100 g	4 oz	4 oz
Can of condensed mushroom soup	300 g	11 oz	I medium
Dried marjoram	5 ml	I tsp	I tsp
Salt and freshly ground black pepper			

① Preheat the slo-cooker on High.

② Heat the oil and butter or margarine in a large frying pan (skillet) and fry (sauté) the onions, garlic and green pepper gently for 2–3 minutes.

③ Stir in the lamb and cook until browned on all sides.

④ Stir in the mushrooms, soup and marjoram and season to taste with salt and pepper. Bring to the boil, then transfer to the slo-cooker.

⑤ Cook on Low for 6–9 hours.

Freezing tip: Cook without the garlic. Add the crushed garlic when reheating.

HONEYED LAMB

—— SERVES 8 ——

	METRIC	IMPERIAL	AMERICAN
Butter or margarine	40 g	1½ oz	3 tbsp
Leg of lamb	2 kg	4½ lb	4½ lb
Salt and freshly ground black pepper			
Cornflour (cornstarch)	15 ml	1 tbsp	1 tbsp
A large pinch of ground ginger			
Dry cider	300 ml	½ pt	1¼ cups
Clear honey	60 ml	4 tbsp	4 tbsp
Rosemary leaves	15 ml	1 tbsp	1 tbsp

①   Preheat the slo-cooker on High.

②   Heat the butter or margarine in a large frying pan (skillet) and brown the lamb on all sides. Season with salt and pepper and transfer to the slo-cooker.

③   Stir the cornflour and ginger into the butter in the pan and mix well, then stir in the cider and honey and bring to the boil, stirring continuously. Pour over the lamb, making sure it is well covered. Sprinkle with the rosemary.

④   Cook on High for 5–7 hours, basting once or twice during cooking if possible.

⑤   Place the joint on a carving dish and serve the sauce separately.

Freezing tip: Leftover slices of lamb can be frozen in a foil tray with some of the sauce poured over.

—— COOKING TIME: **HIGH 5–7 HOURS** ——

NAVARIN OF LAMB
—— SERVES 6–8 ——

	METRIC	IMPERIAL	AMERICAN
Best end of neck of lamb chops	I kg	2¼ lb	2¼ lb
Salt and freshly ground black pepper			
Butter or margarine	15 g	½ oz	I tbsp
Large carrots, sliced	3	3	3
Onions, chopped	2	2	2
Potatoes, cut into I cm/½ in cubes	450 g	I lb	I lb
Plain (all-purpose) flour	30 ml	2 tbsp	2 tbsp
Beef stock	600 ml	I pt	2½ cups
Caster (superfine) sugar	10 ml	2 tsp	2 tsp
Tomato purée (paste)	45 ml	3 tbsp	3 tbsp
Bouquet garni sachet	I	I	I

① Preheat the slo-cooker on High.

② Season the lamb chops with salt and pepper. Melt the butter or margarine in a frying pan (skillet), then brown the chops quickly on both sides. Transfer to the slo-cooker.

③ Add the vegetables to the pan and cook gently for 4 minutes.

④ Mix the flour with a little of the stock, then mix in the remainder. Add to the vegetables in the pan with the remaining ingredients and bring to the boil, stirring continuously. Transfer to the slo-cooker and stir well.

⑤ Cook on Low for 7–10 hours.

⑥ Discard the bouquet garni and adjust the seasoning before serving.

TRADITIONAL LIVER AND BACON
—— SERVES 4 ——

✖	METRIC	IMPERIAL	AMERICAN
Lambs' liver	450 g	1 lb	1 lb
Plain (all-purpose) flour	45 ml	3 tbsp	3 tbsp
Salt and freshly ground black pepper			
Oil	30 ml	2 tbsp	2 tbsp
Back bacon rashers (slices)	8	8	8
Onion, chopped	1	1	1
Beef stock	150 ml	¼ pt	⅔ cup
Butter or margarine	15 g	½ oz	1 tbsp

① Preheat the slo-cooker on High.

② Cut the liver into 1 cm/½ in thick slices. Season 30 ml/ 2 tbsp of the flour with salt and pepper, then toss the liver in the flour, shaking off any excess.

③ Heat the oil in a frying pan (skillet) and fry (sauté) the bacon rashers and onion for 2–3 minutes. Drain off the fat, then transfer the bacon and onion to the slo-cooker.

④ Lightly fry the liver in the pan until just sealed on all sides, then transfer to the slo-cooker.

⑤ Stir the stock into the pan and bring to the boil. Season with salt and pepper, then pour into the slo-cooker.

⑥ Cook on Low for 6–8 hours.

⑦ Blend together the butter or margarine and remaining flour to make a *beurre manié*. Half an hour before the dish is ready, drop pieces of the *beurre manié* into the slo-cooker and stir well to thicken the sauce.

—————— COOKING TIME: **LOW 6–8 HOURS** ——————

PORK IN CIDER

SERVES 4

	METRIC	IMPERIAL	AMERICAN
Oil	15 ml	1 tbsp	1 tbsp
Butter or margarine	25 g	1 oz	2 tbsp
Onion, sliced	1	1	1
Celery sticks, sliced	2	2	2
Large cooking (tart) apple, peeled, cored and chopped	1	1	1
Lean pork, cubed	750 g	1¾ lb	1¾ lb
Plain (all-purpose) flour	30 ml	2 tbsp	2 tbsp
Dry cider	300 ml	½ pt	1¼ cups
Salt and freshly ground black pepper			
Bouquet garni sachet	1	1	1

① Preheat the slo-cooker on High.

② Heat the oil and butter or margarine in a large pan and fry (sauté) the onion, celery and apple gently for 2–3 minutes. Transfer to the slo-cooker.

③ Add the pork to the pan and brown lightly.

④ Mix the flour with a little of the cider, then stir in the rest until well blended. Stir into the pan and bring to the boil, stirring continuously. Transfer to the slo-cooker and stir well. Season with salt and pepper and add the bouquet garni.

⑤ Cook on Low for 6–10 hours.

⑥ Discard the bouquet garni before serving.

COOKING TIME: **LOW 6–10 HOURS**

SWEET AND SOUR PORK CHOPS
—— SERVES 4 ——

✕	METRIC	IMPERIAL	AMERICAN
Plain (all-purpose) flour	15 ml	1 tbsp	1 tbsp
Salt and freshly ground black pepper			
Pork chops, trimmed	4	4	4
Butter or margarine	50 g	2 oz	¼ cup
Onions, finely chopped	2	2	2
Soy sauce	60 ml	4 tbsp	4 tbsp
Tomato purée (paste)	60 ml	4 tbsp	4 tbsp
Soft brown sugar	60 ml	4 tbsp	4 tbsp
Dry sherry	150 ml	¼ pt	⅔ cup

① Preheat the slo-cooker on High.

② Season the flour with salt and pepper, then dust the chops with the flour, shaking off any excess.

③ Heat the butter or margarine in a frying pan (skillet) and brown the chops quickly on all sides. Transfer to the slo-cooker.

④ Add the onions to the pan and fry (sauté) gently until transparent.

⑤ Stir in the remaining ingredients and bring to the boil, then pour over the chops in the slo-cooker.

⑥ Cook on Low for 5–8 hours.

—— COOKING TIME: **LOW 5–8 HOURS** ——

PORK AND PINEAPPLE CURRY

—— SERVES 6 ——

	METRIC	IMPERIAL	AMERICAN
Plain (all-purpose) flour	45 ml	3 tbsp	3 tbsp
Salt	5 ml	1 tsp	1 tsp
Lean pork, cubed	1 kg	2¼ lb	2¼ lb
Oil	30 ml	2 tbsp	2 tbsp
Large onion, finely chopped	1	1	1
Curry powder	15 ml	1 tbsp	1 tbsp
Paprika	15 ml	1 tbsp	1 tbsp
Chicken stock	300 ml	½ pt	1¼ cups
Dried red chillies	2	2	2
Mango chutney	15 ml	1 tbsp	1 tbsp
Worcestershire sauce	5 ml	1 tsp	1 tsp
Can of pineapple cubes in syrup	400 g	14 oz	1 large
Bay leaves	2	2	2
Boiled long-grain rice, to serve			

① Preheat the slo-cooker on High.

② Mix together the flour and salt, then toss the pork pieces in the mixture until coated.

③ Heat the oil in a frying pan (skillet) and brown the meat gently on all sides. Transfer to the slo-cooker.

④ Add the onion to the pan and fry (sauté) until transparent. Add the remaining ingredients and bring to the boil, then transfer to the slo-cooker and stir well.

⑤ Cook on Low for 5–8 hours.

⑥ Discard the bay leaves and stir well. Serve with boiled rice.

SPICED SPARE RIBS

—— SERVES 6 ——

✖	METRIC	IMPERIAL	AMERICAN
Plain (all-purpose) flour	15 ml	1 tbsp	1 tbsp
Salt and freshly ground black pepper			
Pork spare ribs	1 kg	2¼ lb	2¼ lb
Oil	30 ml	2 tbsp	2 tbsp
Onion, finely chopped	1	1	1
Green (bell) pepper, seeded and finely chopped	1	1	1
Garlic clove, crushed	1	1	1
Lager	300 ml	½ pt	1¼ cups
Tomato purée (paste)	30 ml	2 tbsp	2 tbsp
Worcestershire sauce	60 ml	4 tbsp	4 tbsp
A few drops of Tabasco sauce			

① Preheat the slo-cooker on High.

② Season the flour with salt and pepper, then dust the spare ribs with the flour, shaking off any excess.

③ Heat the oil in a frying pan (skillet) and fry (sauté) the spare ribs quickly until browned on all sides. Transfer to the slo-cooker.

④ Add the onion, pepper and garlic to the pan and fry gently for 3–4 minutes.

⑤ Stir in the remaining ingredients, bring to the boil, then pour over the ribs in the slo-cooker.

⑥ Cook on Low for 6–8 hours.

—————— COOKING TIME: **LOW 6–8 HOURS** ——————

EASY CASSOULET

—— SERVES 4 ——

⚠ ❄

	METRIC	IMPERIAL	AMERICAN
Dried haricot (navy) beans	450 g	I lb	I lb
Bay leaf, crushed	I	I	I
Garlic cloves, crushed	2	2	2
Dried thyme	2.5 ml	½ tsp	½ tsp
Dried sage	2.5 ml	½ tsp	½ tsp
Salt and freshly ground black pepper			
Belly pork, rinded and cubed	450 g	I lb	lb
Toulouse or other spicy sausages	350 g	12 oz	12 oz
Chicken stock	250 ml	8 fl oz	I cup
Fresh breadcrumbs	100 g	4 oz	2 cups
Strong cheese, grated	50 g	2 oz	½ cup
To thicken (optional):			
Plain (all-purpose) flour	15 ml	I tbsp	I tbsp
Butter or margarine	15 ml	I tbsp	I tbsp

① Preheat the slo-cooker on High.

② Place the beans in the slo-cooker and cover with cold water. Cook on Low overnight until soft.

③ Drain the beans, then return to the slo-cooker with the bay leaf, garlic, thyme, sage and seasoning.

④ Heat a frying pan (skillet) and fry (sauté) the pork until sealed on all sides. Stir into the beans.

⑤ In the same pan, fry the sausages until lightly browned, then place on top of the beans.

⑥ Pour the stock into the pan, bring to the boil, then pour into the slo-cooker. Cook on Low for 8–10 hours.

⑦ If you wish to thicken the cassoulet, half an hour before serving mix together the flour and butter to make a *beurre manié* and stir it into the cassoulet.

⑧ Mix together the breadcrumbs and cheese and sprinkle over the cassoulet. Brown under a hot grill (broiler) for a few minutes before serving.

—— COOKING TIME: **LOW 8–10 HOURS** ——

PIQUANT BACON
—— SERVES 6 ——

✗ ❄	METRIC	IMPERIAL	AMERICAN
Unsmoked bacon, rinded and cubed	1 kg	2¼ lb	2¼ lb
Butter or margarine	50 g	2 oz	¼ cup
Large onion, chopped	1	1	1
Carrots, sliced	2	2	2
Plain (all-purpose) flour	30 ml	2 tbsp	2 tbsp
Chicken stock or dry white wine	300 ml	½ pt	1¼ cups
Wine vinegar	45 ml	3 tbsp	3 tbsp
Freshly ground black pepper	2.5 ml	½ tsp	½ tsp
A pinch of ground cloves			

① Preheat the slo-cooker on High.

② Place the bacon cubes in a saucepan and cover with cold water. Bring slowly to the boil. Discard the water and pat the bacon dry on kitchen paper (paper towels).

③ Heat the butter or margarine in a frying pan (skillet) and brown the bacon lightly on all sides. Transfer to the slo-cooker.

④ Add the onion and carrots to the frying pan and fry (sauté) for a few minutes. Stir in the flour, then gradually add the chicken stock or wine and the vinegar. Bring to the boil, then add the pepper and cloves. Transfer to the slo-cooker and stir well.

⑤ Cook on Low for 7–10 hours.

—————— COOKING TIME: **LOW 7–10 HOURS** ——————

BRAISED BACON WITH TOMATOES

—— SERVES 6 ——

	METRIC	IMPERIAL	AMERICAN
Collar or gammon bacon joint	1 kg	2¼ lb	2¼ lb
Brown sugar	15 ml	1 tbsp	1 tbsp
Tomatoes, skinned and coarsely chopped	225 g	8 oz	8 oz
Onions, thinly sliced	225 g	8 oz	8 oz
Freshly ground black pepper			
Water	30 ml	2 tbsp	2 tbsp
Button mushrooms, sliced	100 g	4 oz	4 oz
Water	30 ml	2 tbsp	2 tbsp
Lemon juice	30 ml	2 tbsp	2 tbsp
Chopped parsley	15 ml	1 tbsp	1 tbsp

① Preheat the slo-cooker on High.

② Place the bacon in a saucepan and cover with cold water. Bring slowly to the boil, then discard the water and remove the bacon from the pan.

③ Cut off the rind and snip the remaining fat at intervals. Sprinkle the joint with the brown sugar and place under a preheated grill (broiler) to melt and brown.

④ Layer the tomato and onion slices in the slo-cooker, season with pepper and add the water. Place the browned bacon joint on top.

⑤ Cook on High for 3–5 hours.

⑥ In a separate saucepan, cook the mushrooms with the water and lemon juice for about 4 minutes, then drain.

⑦ Garnish the bacon with the mushrooms and parsley and serve.

Freezing tip: Freeze without the mushroom and parsley garnish.

—— COOKING TIME: **HIGH 3–5 HOURS** ——

POULTRY & GAME

Slo-cooking poultry and game guarantees that it remains moist and tender, with none of the drying out that can take place during conventional cooking. You can cook whole birds, joints or pieces, and the slo-cooker will tenderise even the toughest birds without any loss of flavour.

The size of your slo-cooker will obviously determine the size of bird you will be able to cook. A 2.5 litre/4½ pint pot will accommodate a 1.75 kg/4 lb bird.

Thaw frozen poultry completely before slo-cooking. Frozen poultry dishes are best defrosted at room temperature, then reheated gently in the oven just before serving.

POULTRY AND GAME TIPS

◇ Always cook whole birds on High.

◇ Avoid overcooking as the bones will begin to fall apart if the dish is left to cook for too long.

◇ Light browning before cooking will improve both the flavour and appearance of poultry dishes.

◇ Whole birds are best trussed so that they can easily be removed from the pot when cooked.

◇ Make sure that vegetables are cut into small pieces so that they cook in time.

◇ Season lightly before cooking, then adjust the seasoning before serving.

◇ Use about half the liquid specified in conventional recipes if you adapt them for the slo-cooker.

◇ You can use stock, water, wine, cider or fruit juice for slo-cooking poultry.

◇ Thicken dishes before cooking or for the last 1–1½ hours (see page 11).

◇ Add egg yolks, cream or milk for only the last 30 minutes of cooking.

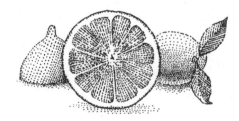

CHILLI AND GINGER CHICKEN
—— SERVES 4 ——

✖ ❄

	METRIC	IMPERIAL	AMERICAN
Butter or margarine	50 g	2 oz	¼ cup
Chicken portions	4	4	4
Onion, chopped	1	1	1
Celery sticks, chopped	2	2	2
Plain (all-purpose) flour	30 ml	2 tbsp	2 tbsp
Chicken stock	150 ml	¼ pt	⅔ cup
Can of pineapple pieces in juice	450 g	14 oz	1 large
Chilli powder	10 ml	2 tsp	2 tsp
Ground ginger	2.5 ml	½ tsp	½ tsp
A few drops of Tabasco sauce			
Salt and freshly ground black pepper			

① Preheat the slo-cooker on High.

② Heat the butter or margarine in a frying pan (skillet) and brown the chicken portions on all sides. Transfer to the slo-cooker.

③ Add the onion and celery to the pan and fry (sauté) until transparent.

④ Stir in the flour, then gradually stir in the stock, the pineapple and juice and the remaining ingredients and bring to the boil, stirring continuously. Pour over the chicken.

⑤ Cook on Low for 5–8 hours.

—— COOKING TIME: **LOW 5–8 HOURS** ——

CURRIED CHICKEN LEGS

—— SERVES 4 ——

✕ ❄	METRIC	IMPERIAL	AMERICAN
Oil	30 ml	2 tbsp	2 tbsp
Chicken legs, skinned	4	4	4
Salt and freshly ground black pepper			
Onion, chopped	1	1	1
Garlic clove, crushed	1	1	1
Sultanas (golden raisins)	50 g	2 oz	⅓ cup
Curry powder	30 ml	2 tbsp	2 tbsp
Plain (all-purpose) flour	30 ml	2 tbsp	2 tbsp
Chicken stock	150 ml	¼ pt	⅔ cup
Naan bread and spicy Indian chutneys, to serve			

① Preheat the slo-cooker on High.

② Heat the oil in a frying pan (skillet) and lightly brown the chicken legs on all sides. Remove from the pan with a slotted spoon, season with salt and pepper and place in the slo-cooker.

③ Add the onion and garlic to the pan and fry (sauté) until transparent, then stir in the sultanas. Transfer to the slo-cooker.

④ Stir the curry powder and flour into the pan and fry gently for 2 minutes, stirring continuously. Gradually add the stock, stirring all the time, and bring to the boil, then pour into the slo-cooker.

⑤ Cook on Low for 6–8 hours.

⑥ Serve with naan bread and spicy Indian chutnies.

—————— COOKING TIME: **LOW 6–8 HOURS** ——————

COQ AU VIN

— SERVES 4 —

	METRIC	IMPERIAL	AMERICAN
Butter or margarine	50 g	2 oz	¼ cup
Chicken portions, skinned	4	4	4
Onions, chopped	2	2	2
Garlic clove, crushed	1	1	1
Streaky bacon rashers (slices), rinded and chopped	4	4	4
Button mushrooms, halved	100 g	4 oz	4 oz
Plain (all-purpose) flour	50 g	2 oz	½ cup
Chicken stock	150 ml	¼ pt	⅔ cup
Red wine	300 ml	½ pt	1¼ cups
Bay leaves	2	2	2
Bouquet garni sachet	1	1	1
Salt and freshly ground black pepper			

① Preheat the slo-cooker on High.

② Heat the butter or margarine in a frying pan (skillet) and brown the chicken pieces on all sides. Transfer to the slo-cooker.

③ Add the onion, garlic and bacon to the pan and fry (sauté) gently until transparent.

④ Stir in the mushrooms, then the flour and cook for 1 minute, then stir in the stock and wine and bring to the boil. Add the bay leaves and bouquet garni and season with salt and pepper. Transfer to the slo-cooker.

⑤ Cook on Low for 6–8 hours.

⑥ Discard the bay leaves and bouquet garni before serving.

COOKING TIME: **LOW 6–8 HOURS**

CHICKEN CASSEROLE
—— SERVES 4 ——

� ❄

	METRIC	IMPERIAL	AMERICAN
Butter or margarine	50 g	2 oz	¼ cup
Chicken portions	4	4	4
Onions, chopped	2	2	2
Garlic clove, crushed	1	1	1
Streaky bacon rashers (slices), rinded and chopped	2	2	2
Carrots, chopped	2	2	2
Celery sticks, chopped	2	2	2
Plain (all-purpose) flour	30 ml	2 tbsp	2 tbsp
Chicken stock	450 ml	¾ pt	2 cups
Tomato purée (paste)	30 ml	2 tbsp	2 tbsp
Bouquet garni sachet	1	1	1
Salt and freshly ground black pepper			
Mixed frozen sweetcorn (corn) and chopped (bell) peppers	225 g	8 oz	8 oz

① Preheat the slo-cooker on High.

② Heat the butter or margarine in a frying pan (skillet) and brown the chicken on all sides. Transfer to the slo-cooker.

③ Add the onions, garlic, bacon, carrots and celery to the pan and fry (sauté) for 4 minutes.

④ Stir in the flour, then gradually stir in the stock, tomato purée, bouquet garni and seasoning and bring to the boil, stirring continuously. Pour over the chicken.

⑤ Cook on Low for 6–8 hours.

⑥ About 30 minutes before serving, stir in the sweetcorn and peppers.

⑦ Discard the bouquet garni and adjust the seasoning before serving.

Freezer tip: Omit the garlic when slo-cooking, then add the garlic or season with garlic salt when reheating.

—————— COOKING TIME: **LOW 6–8 HOURS** ——————

PARSLEY ROAST CHICKEN

—— SERVES 6 ——

⚠ ❄

	METRIC	IMPERIAL	AMERICAN
Whole chicken	1.75 kg	4 lb	4 lb
Garlic cloves, cut into slivers	2	2	2
Salt and freshly ground black pepper			
Oil	60 ml	4 tbsp	4 tbsp
Butter or margarine	100 g	4 oz	½ cup
Chopped parsley	45 ml	3 tbsp	3 tbsp

① Preheat the slo-cooker on High.

② Using a sharp knife, cut small slits in the breasts and thighs of the chicken and insert the slivers of garlic. Season the bird with salt and pepper.

③ Heat the oil and butter or margarine in a large frying pan (skillet) and brown the chicken on all sides. Transfer the chicken to the slo-cooker.

④ Stir the parsley into the remaining butter or margarine in the pan, then pour over the chicken.

⑤ Cook on High for 4–5 hours.

⑥ Cover with foil and leave to rest for a few minutes before carving.

—— COOKING TIME: **HIGH 4–5 HOURS** ——

CHICKEN AND PEPPER RISOTTO

—— SERVES 4 ——

✕ ①	METRIC	IMPERIAL	AMERICAN
Oil	30 ml	2 tbsp	2 tbsp
Onions, finely chopped	2	2	2
Chicken stock	900 ml	1½ pts	3¾ cups
Small green (bell) pepper, seeded and chopped	1	1	1
Small red (bell) pepper, seeded and chopped	1	1	1
Button mushrooms	100 g	4 oz	4 oz
Tomatoes, skinned and chopped	3	3	3
Easy-cook medium- or long-grain rice	175 g	6 oz	¾ cup
Cooked chicken, chopped	225 g	8 oz	2 cups
Cooked ham, chopped	50 g	2 oz	½ cup
Parmesan cheese, freshly grated	50 g	2 oz	½ cup

① Preheat the slo-cooker on High.

② Heat the oil in a large frying pan (skillet) and fry (sauté) the onions until transparent.

③ Add the stock and bring to the boil. Stir in the remaining ingredients except the Parmesan and return to the boil, then transfer to the slo-cooker.

④ Cook on Low for 3–4 hours.

⑤ Stir well before serving sprinkled with the Parmesan.

—— COOKING TIME: **LOW 3–4 HOURS** ——

BAKED LEMON AND CREAM CHICKEN

—— SERVES 4 ——

✗ ❄

	METRIC	IMPERIAL	AMERICAN
Chicken breasts, skinned	4	4	4
Garlic clove, cut into slivers	1	1	1
Grated rind and juice of lemon	1	1	1
Salt and freshly ground black pepper			
Butter or margarine	25 g	1 oz	2 tbsp
Oil	30 ml	2 tbsp	2 tbsp
Single (light) cream	30 ml	2 tbsp	2 tbsp
Chopped parsley	15 ml	1 tbsp	1 tbsp

① Preheat the slo-cooker on High.

② Make small cuts in the chicken breasts and insert slivers of garlic and a little lemon rind. Season the breasts with salt and pepper.

③ Heat the butter or margarine and oil in a frying pan (skillet) and brown the chicken breasts quickly on all sides. Lift from the pan into the slo-cooker.

④ Stir the lemon juice into the pan and bring to the boil, then pour over the chicken.

⑤ Cook on Low for 6–8 hours.

⑥ Half an hour before serving, stir in the cream and parsley.

COOKING TIME: **LOW 6–8 HOURS**

CHINESE CHICKEN WITH PINEAPPLE

—— SERVES 4 ——

✂ ❄	METRIC	IMPERIAL	AMERICAN
Chicken pieces, skinned	4	4	4
Salt and freshly ground black pepper			
Oil	30 ml	2 tbsp	2 tbsp
Onion, chopped	1	1	1
Red (bell) pepper, seeded and chopped	1	1	1
Chicken stock	300 ml	½ pt	1¼ cups
Soft brown sugar	15 ml	1 tbsp	1 tbsp
Soy sauce	15 ml	1 tbsp	1 tbsp
Ground ginger	2.5 ml	½ tsp	½ tsp
Can of pineapple cubes, drained	300 g	11 oz	1 medium
Cornflour (cornstarch)	10 ml	2 tsp	2 tsp

1. Preheat the slo-cooker on High.
2. Season the chicken with salt and pepper. Heat the oil in a frying pan (skillet) and brown the chicken quickly on all sides, then transfer to the slo-cooker.
3. Stir all the remaining ingredients except the cornflour into the pan, stir together well and heat through, then transfer to the slo-cooker.
4. Cook on Low for 8–10 hours.
5. Half an hour before serving, blend the cornflour with a little water, then stir it into the slo-cooker to thicken the sauce.

—— COOKING TIME: **LOW 8–10 HOURS** ——

PAELLA

—— SERVES 6 ——

✂ ①

	METRIC	IMPERIAL	AMERICAN
Oil	30 ml	2 tbsp	2 tbsp
Onion, finely chopped	1	1	1
Garlic clove, crushed	1	1	1
Chicken stock	900 ml	1½ pts	3¾ cups
A pinch of ground saffron			
Easy-cook long-grain rice	225 g	8 oz	1 cup
Tomatoes, skinned and chopped	4	4	4
Red (bell) pepper, seeded and finely chopped	1	1	1
Cooked chicken, chopped	225 g	8 oz	2 cups
Salt and freshly ground black pepper			
Cooked mussels	6	6	6
Cooked prawns (shrimp)	6	6	6
Frozen peas, thawed	100 g	4 oz	4 oz

① Preheat the slo-cooker on High.

② Heat the oil in a large frying pan (skillet) and fry (sauté) the onion and garlic until transparent.

③ Add the stock and saffron, bring to the boil, then stir in all the remaining ingredients except the mussels, prawns and peas. Season with salt and pepper. Return to the boil, then transfer to the slo-cooker.

④ Cook on Low for 3–4 hours.

⑤ Half an hour before serving, stir in the mussels prawns and peas.

—— COOKING TIME: **LOW 3–4 HOURS** ——

PHEASANT IN CIDER

—— SERVES 4 ——

⚠	METRIC	IMPERIAL	AMERICAN
Plain (all-purpose) flour	30 ml	2 tbsp	2 tbsp
Salt and freshly ground black pepper			
Large pheasant	I	I	I
Butter or margarine	50 g	2 oz	¼ cup
Onion, finely chopped	I	I	I
Garlic clove, crushed	I	I	I
Dry cider	300 ml	½ pt	I¼ cups
Bouquet garni sachet	I	I	I
Streaky bacon rashers (slices), rinded	4	4	4
Eating (dessert) apples	2	2	2
Lemon juice	I5 ml	I tbsp	I tbsp
Soured (dairy sour) cream	60 ml	4 tbsp	4 tbsp
Paprika	5 ml	I tsp	I tsp

① Preheat the slo-cooker on High.

② Season the flour with salt and pepper. Dust the pheasant in half the flour, shaking off any excess.

③ Heat half the butter or margarine in a large frying pan (skillet) and quickly brown the pheasant on all sides. Transfer to the slo-cooker.

④ In the same pan, fry (sauté) the onion and garlic gently until transparent.

⑤ Stir in the remaining flour and cook for 1 minute, then gradually stir in the cider and bring to the boil. Add the bouquet garni and season with salt and pepper. Pour over the pheasant.

⑥ Cook on High for 3–4 hours.

⑦ Lift the pheasant from the slo-cooker, cover with foil and leave to rest.

⑧ Heat the remaining butter or margarine in a pan. Roll up the bacon rashers and fry in the butter until crisp.

⑨   Peel, core and quarter the apples and immediately toss in the lemon juice. Add to the pan and fry until golden.

⑩   Strain the pheasant cooking juices and reheat in a pan, then stir in the soured cream and paprika but do not allow the mixture to boil.

⑪   Serve the pheasant garnished with the sauce, bacon and apples.

TURKEY IN A CREAM SAUCE

— SERVES 6 —

	METRIC	IMPERIAL	AMERICAN
Butter or margarine	25 g	1 oz	2 tbsp
Turkey meat, cubed	450 g	1 lb	1 lb
Onion, thinly sliced	1	1	1
Celery sticks, chopped	3	3	3
Carrots, chopped	2	2	2
Plain (all-purpose) flour	30 ml	2 tbsp	2 tbsp
Chicken stock	300 ml	½ pt	1¼ cups
Bouquet garni sachet	1	1	1
Salt and freshly ground black pepper			
Single (light) cream	150 ml	¼ pt	⅔ cup

① Preheat the slo-cooker on High.

② Heat the butter or margarine in a frying pan (skillet) and fry (sauté) the turkey gently until sealed on all sides, then transfer to the slo-cooker.

③ Add the onion, celery and carrots to the pan and fry for 3–4 minutes.

④ Stir in the flour and cook for 1 minute, then gradually stir in the stock and bring to the boil. Add the bouquet garni and season with salt and pepper. Pour over the turkey.

⑤ Cook on Low for 6–8 hours.

⑥ Half an hour before serving, stir in the cream.

Freezing tip: Freeze without the cream. Stir in the cream during reheating.

COOKING TIME: **LOW 6–8 HOURS**

VEGETABLES & VEGETARIAN

Vegetable flavours are delicate, so it is good to know that the flavours are sealed during slo-cooking and gently but surely developed within the pot. You may find that the texture differs slightly from vegetables cooked conventionally but you will most certainly note and appreciate the improved flavours. Fresh, frozen and dried vegetables are all suitable for slo-cooking.

Some of the recipes in this chapter are suitable for main dishes, others will make delicious side dishes or starters.

Frozen vegetables should be thawed before adding to the slo-cooker. In order to retain their full colour and texture, stir them into a recipe during the final 30 minutes of cooking. This will also avoid suddenly and drastically lowering the temperature within the slo-cooker.

Slo-cooked vegetables can be frozen, particularly if cooked in a sauce, though you may not feel it is worth it for some recipes. Remember that vegetables tend to lose some of their flavour and texture on freezing and reheating.

VEGETABLE TIPS

◇ Vegetables generally require a longer cooking time in the slo-cooker than when cooked conventionally. Cut them into small pieces about 5 mm/¼ in thick, particularly in recipes that combine vegetables and meat. Try to ensure that the pieces are of even size.

◇ Root vegetables such as potatoes, carrots, turnips, swede (rutabaga) and onions usually require a cooking time of at least six hours on Low.

◇ Vegetables, especially potatoes, should be just covered in liquid while slo-cooking.

◇ Pre-cooked vegetables can be added to a recipe 30 minutes before serving.

◇ Do not over-season as vegetables will retain all their concentrated flavours. Check and adjust the seasoning before serving.

◇ When adapting conventional recipes, reduce the amount of liquid used. You may also need to reduce the quantity of strongly flavoured vegetables, such as leeks or onions.

◇ Thickening agents such as flour and cornflour (cornstarch) can be added at the start of cooking (see page 11). Add cream, milk or egg yolks during the final 30 minutes.

◇ If a recipe includes dried peas or beans, they should be soaked overnight in cold water before cooking. Drain and rinse the beans, then cover in fresh water and boil rapidly for 15 minutes to destroy any natural toxins in the pulses. Always season after cooking as salt causes the beans to harden during cooking. Soaking is not necessary for lentils.

◇ Canned pulses should be drained and rinsed, then added for the final 30 minutes of cooking.

◇ Cheese and other dairy products are used in this chapter, so strict vegetarians should make sure they use suitable vegetarian products.

COURGETTES HEREFORD

—— SERVES 4–6 ——

	METRIC	IMPERIAL	AMERICAN
Butter or margarine	40 g	1½ oz	3 tbsp
Courgettes (zucchini), cut into 2.5 cm/1 in lengths	450 g	1 lb	1 lb
Garlic clove, crushed	1	1	1
Small onion, finely chopped	1	1	1
Cornflour (cornstarch)	15 ml	1 tbsp	1 tbsp
Apple juice	300 ml	½ pt	1¼ cups
Salt and freshly ground black pepper			
Tomatoes, skinned and sliced	3	3	3

①   Preheat the slo-cooker on High.

②   Heat the butter or margarine in a frying pan (skillet) and fry (sauté) the courgettes quickly until lightly browned. Transfer to the slo-cooker.

③   In the same fat, fry the garlic and onion gently until transparent. Add the cornflour, then carefully stir in the apple juice. Season with salt and pepper, stir in the tomatoes and bring to the boil, stirring continuously. Pour the sauce over the courgettes.

④   Cook on Low for 4–6 hours until the courgettes are tender but still have a slight bite.

—————— COOKING TIME: **LOW 4–6 HOURS** ——————

GREEK MUSHROOMS

—— SERVES 8 ——

✕ ❄	METRIC	IMPERIAL	AMERICAN
Oil	30 ml	2 tbsp	2 tbsp
Onion, finely chopped	1	1	1
Garlic clove, crushed	1	1	1
Button mushrooms	450 g	1 lb	1 lb
Chestnut mushrooms	225 g	8 oz	8 oz
Can of tomatoes	400 g	14 oz	1 large
Salt and freshly ground black pepper			
Chopped parsley	15 ml	1 tbsp	1 tbsp

① Preheat the slo-cooker on High.

② Heat the oil in a frying pan (skillet) and fry (sauté) the onion and garlic gently until transparent. Add the mushrooms and tomatoes and season with salt and pepper. Bring to the boil, then transfer to the slo-cooker.

③ Cook on Low for 2–3 hours.

④ Stir in the parsley before serving.

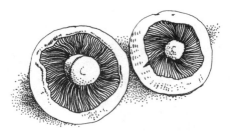

CREAMED CHEESE AND ONION POTATOES

—— SERVES 4 ——

✗	METRIC	IMPERIAL	AMERICAN
Butter or margarine	25 g	1 oz	2 tbsp
Streaky bacon, rinded and chopped	100 g	4 oz	4 oz
Onion, finely chopped	1	1	1
Garlic clove, crushed	1	1	1
Cheddar cheese, grated	100 g	4 oz	1 cup
Chopped parsley	15 ml	1 tbsp	1 tbsp
Salt and freshly ground black pepper			
Potatoes, thinly sliced	900 g	2 lb	2 lb
Milk	450 ml	¾ pt	2 cups
Eggs, beaten	2	2	2

① Rub the butter or margarine over the slo-cooker pot, then preheat on High.

② Fry (sauté) the bacon in a frying pan (skillet) until crisp. Remove with a slotted spoon.

③ Fry the onion in the bacon fat until just beginning to soften, then remove from the heat and stir in the cooked bacon, the garlic, cheese and parsley and season with salt and pepper.

④ Arrange a layer of potatoes in the base of the slo-cooker and sprinkle with salt and pepper. Cover with a layer of the cheese and onion mixture, then repeat until all the ingredients have been used up, finishing with a layer of cheese.

⑤ Heat the milk but do not allow it to boil. Beat in the eggs, then pour over the potatoes.

⑥ Cook on Low for 8–9 hours.

RATATOUILLE
—— SERVES 4 ——

✕ ❄

	METRIC	IMPERIAL	AMERICAN
Olive oil	120 ml	4 fl oz	½ cup
Large onion, finely chopped	1	1	1
Green (bell) pepper, seeded and sliced	1	1	1
Red (bell) pepper, seeded and sliced	1	1	1
Large aubergine (eggplant), diced	1	1	1
Courgettes (zucchini), thickly sliced	3	3	3
Tomatoes, skinned, seeded and chopped	450 g	1 lb	1 lb
OR Can of chopped tomatoes	400 g	14 oz	1 large
Garlic cloves, crushed	2	2	2
Salt and freshly ground black pepper			
A few basil leaves, torn			
Chopped parsley	15 ml	1 tbsp	1 tbsp

① Preheat the slo-cooker on High.

② Heat the oil in a large frying pan (skillet) or saucepan and fry the onion and peppers until soft but not browned.

③ Add all the remaining ingredients except the herbs and season with salt and pepper. Heat through, turning the vegetables thoroughly in the oil. Transfer to the slo-cooker.

④ Cook on Low for 5–8 hours.

⑤ Stir in the basil and parsley and serve hot or cold as a side dish or starter.

BAKED CHEESE ONIONS

— SERVES 4 —

	METRIC	IMPERIAL	AMERICAN
Onions	4	4	4
Strong cheese, grated	100 g	4 oz	1 cup
Fresh breadcrumbs	50 g	2 oz	1 cup
Salt and freshly ground black pepper			
Hot vegetable stock	150 ml	¼ pt	⅔ cup

① Preheat the slo-cooker on High.

② Peel the onions and cut the base flat so that they stand upright. Place in a pan, cover with water, bring to the boil, then boil for 3 minutes. Drain well and remove the cores. You can use the cores for another recipe, or chop them and add them to the stuffing.

③ Mix together the cheese and breadcrumbs and season with salt and pepper. Mix in the chopped onion cores, if using. Stuff into the centres of the onions, pressing down firmly. Stand the onions in the slo-cooker and pour over the stock.

④ Cook on Low for 6–8 hours.

⑤ Serve as a side dish or a main course with salad.

COOKING TIME: **LOW 6–8 HOURS**

PEPPER AND NUT RICE

—— SERVES 4 ——

✗	METRIC	IMPERIAL	AMERICAN
Olive oil	15 ml	I tbsp	I tbsp
Onion, finely chopped	I	I	I
Easy-cook long-grain rice	225 g	8 oz	I cup
Red (bell) pepper, seeded and chopped	I	I	I
Walnuts, coarsely chopped	50 g	2 oz	½ cup
Almonds, coarsely chopped	50 g	2 oz	½ cup
Peanuts, coarsely chopped	50 g	2 oz	½ cup
Sultanas (golden raisins)	50 g	2 oz	⅓ cup
Vegetable stock	300 ml	½ pt	I ¼ cups
Salt and freshly ground black pepper			

① Preheat the slo-cooker on High.

② Heat the oil in a frying pan (skillet) and fry the onion until transparent. Stir in all the remaining ingredients, seasoning with salt and pepper. Transfer to the slo-cooker.

③ Cook on Low for 6–8 hours.

④ Serve as a side dish or as a main dish with salad.

—————— COOKING TIME: **LOW 6–8 HOURS** ——————

ITALIAN STUFFED PEPPERS

—— SERVES 4 ——

⚠	METRIC	IMPERIAL	AMERICAN
Quick-cook thin macaroni	50 g	2 oz	2 oz
Salt			
Oil	30 ml	2 tbsp	2 tbsp
Onion, diced	I	I	I
Garlic clove, crushed	I	I	I
Minced (ground) Quorn	450 g	I lb	I lb
Plain (all-purpose) flour	30 ml	2 tbsp	2 tbsp
Tomato purée (paste)	15 ml	I tbsp	I tbsp
Tomato ketchup (catsup)	15 ml	I tbsp	I tbsp
Vegetable stock	150 ml	¼ pt	⅔ cup
Button mushrooms, diced	100 g	4 oz	4 oz
Dried mixed herbs	5 ml	I tsp	I tsp
Large green or red (bell) peppers	4	4	4
Boiling water	150 ml	¼ pt	⅔ cup

① Preheat the slo-cooker on High.

② Boil the macaroni in lightly salted water until just tender. Drain.

③ Heat the oil in a frying pan (skillet) and fry (sauté) the onion and garlic until transparent.

④ Add the Quorn and continue to cook, stirring for 3 minutes. Stir in the flour, tomato purée, tomato ketchup and stock. Bring to the boil and boil until thickened, stirring continuously. Add the mushrooms, herbs and drained macaroni.

⑤ Remove the stalk and cut the cap from the top of each pepper. Remove the seeds and membranes. Fill the peppers with the mixture and stand them in the slo-cooker, without allowing them to touch the walls. Pour round the water and add a pinch of salt.

⑥ Cook on Low for 5–8 hours.

⑦ Serve as a side dish or a main dish with rice or pasta.

—————— COOKING TIME: **LOW 5–8 HOURS** ——————

TUNA-STUFFED MARROW

—— SERVES 6 ——

⚠	METRIC	IMPERIAL	AMERICAN
Can of tuna, drained and flaked	200 g	7 oz	I small
Onion, finely chopped	I	I	I
Cooked long-grain rice	60 ml	4 tbsp	4 tbsp
Chopped parsley	15 ml	I tbsp	I tbsp
Juice of lemon	I	I	I
Salt and freshly ground black pepper			
Medium marrow (squash)	I	I	I
Butter or margarine	25 g	I oz	2 tbsp
Boiling water	300 ml	½ pt	I¼ cups
Tomato sauce or ketchup (catsup), to serve			

① Preheat the slo-cooker on High.

② Mix the tuna with the onion, rice, parsley and lemon juice and season with salt and pepper.

③ Cut the ends off the marrow so it will stand upright in the slo-cooker, then scoop out the seeds. Fill the marrow with the mixture and wrap in buttered foil. Stand the marrow in the slo-cooker and pour the water around.

④ Cook on Low for 8–10 hours.

⑤ Serve hot with tomato sauce as a main or side dish.

MACARONI CHEESE

—— SERVES 4 ——

✗	METRIC	IMPERIAL	AMERICAN
Butter or margarine	15 g	1 oz	2 tbsp
Quick-cook macaroni	175 g	6 oz	6 oz
Salt and freshly ground black pepper			
White Sauce (page 34)	300 ml	½ pt	1¼ cups
Cheddar cheese, grated	175 g	6 oz	1½ cups
A large pinch of cayenne			

① Rub the inside of the slo-cooker with the butter or margarine, then preheat on High.

② Bring a large pan of lightly salted water to the boil, add the macaroni and stir well as it returns to the boil. Boil rapidly for 2 minutes, then drain well.

③ Make the white sauce, then remove from the heat and stir in three-quarters of the cheese. Season with cayenne, salt and pepper. Mix the macaroni with the sauce and transfer to the slo-cooker. Sprinkle with the remaining cheese.

④ Cook on Low for 3–4 hours.

⑤ Serve as a side dish or main course.

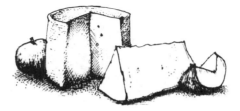

—— COOKING TIME: **LOW 3–4 HOURS** ——

LEEK AND CIDER HOTPOT

—— SERVES 6 ——

✖ ❋

	METRIC	IMPERIAL	AMERICAN
Butter or margarine	50 g	2 oz	¼ cup
Bacon, rinded and chopped	100 g	4 oz	4 oz
Leeks, chopped	900 g	2 lb	2 lb
Eating (dessert) apples, peeled, cored and sliced	2	2	2
Dry cider	600 ml	1 pt	2½ cups
Plain (all-purpose) flour	45 ml	3 tbsp	3 tbsp

① Preheat the slo-cooker on High.

② Heat the butter or margarine in a large frying pan (skillet) and fry (sauté) the bacon for 3 minutes. Stir in the leeks and apples and toss together well.

③ Mix a little of the cider with the flour to make a smooth paste, then blend in the remaining cider. Add to the pan and bring to the boil, stirring continuously. Transfer to the slo-cooker.

④ Cook on Low for 6–10 hours.

⑤ Serve as a side dish or main course with steamed vegetables.

—————— COOKING TIME: **LOW 6–10 HOURS**——————

STUFFED AUBERGINES

—— SERVES 4 ——

	METRIC	IMPERIAL	AMERICAN
Aubergines (eggplants), halved lengthways	2	2	2
Salt and freshly ground black pepper			
Olive oil	60 ml	4 tbsp	4 tbsp
Onion, chopped	I	I	I
Garlic clove, crushed	I	I	I
Tomatoes, skinned and chopped	I	I	I
Chopped parsley	15 ml	I tbsp	I tbsp
Hot vegetable stock	150 ml	¼ pt	⅔ cup
Fresh breadcrumbs	50 g	2 oz	I cup
Strong cheese, grated	50 g	2 oz	½ cup

① Sprinkle the aubergines with salt and leave to stand for 1 hour. Rinse and drain well.

② Preheat the slo-cooker on High.

③ Heat the oil in a large frying pan (skillet) and fry (sauté) the aubergines, cut-side down, until soft. Remove from the pan and scoop out the flesh, leaving the shells intact. Chop the flesh.

④ Fry the onion in the remaining oil until transparent, then remove from the heat and stir in the chopped aubergine, the garlic, tomatoes and parsley. Season with salt and pepper. Pile into the aubergine shells, place them in the slo-cooker and pour around the hot stock.

⑤ Cook on Low for 4–6 hours.

⑥ Mix together the breadcrumbs and cheese and sprinkle over the aubergines. Brown under a hot grill (broiler) before serving.

⑦ Serve as a side dish or main course with rice or salad.

WINTER POTATO CASSEROLE

—— SERVES 4–6 ——

✕	METRIC	IMPERIAL	AMERICAN
Butter or margarine	50 g	2 oz	¼ cup
Small onion, finely chopped	1	1	1
Garlic clove, crushed	1	1	1
Carrot, chopped	1	1	1
Celery stick, finely chopped	1	1	1
Potatoes, diced	450 g	1 lb	1 lb
Ground mace	2.5 ml	½ tsp	½ tsp
Salt and freshly ground black pepper			
Can of condensed cream of chicken soup	300 g	11 oz	1 medium
Water	150 ml	¼ pt	⅔ cup

① Preheat the slo-cooker on High.

② Heat the butter or margarine in a large frying pan (skillet) and fry the onion, garlic, carrot, celery and potatoes for 5 minutes. Season with the mace and salt and pepper.

③ Mix together the soup and water, pour into the pan and bring to the boil, stirring continuously. Transfer to the slo-cooker.

④ Cook on Low for 6–8 hours.

⑤ Serve as a main course with steamed vegetables.

—————— COOKING TIME: **LOW 6–8 HOURS** ——————

DESSERTS & CAKES

Those delightful nursery puddings need no longer be just memories of childhood. They can easily be adapted for slo-cooking and come out perfectly every time.

Slo-cooked fruit is something special. Its flavour is gently developed within the pot while the fruit remains beautifully whole for serving. Or you can use the slo-cooker to make pie, pudding and crumble fillings while you are busy with other tasks.

Delicate desserts, such as egg custard, that require long, slow cooking are ideal for the slo-cooker as there is no danger of them overcooking and spoiling.

Sponge puddings can be frozen raw or cooked but suet puddings are best frozen raw. Cooked fruits can also be frozen, as can pie fillings. Leftover sponge pudding can be frozen, then covered with foil in an ovenproof dish and reheated in the slo-cooker surrounded with water on Low for 1–2 hours. Egg custards and similar puddings are not suitable for freezing.

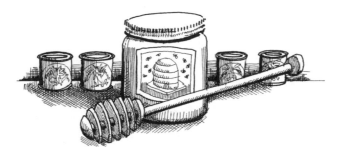

DESSERT TIPS

◇ Dried fruit must be covered with liquid if it is to cook evenly.

◇ Fill steamed pudding basins only two-thirds full and make a pleat in the greaseproof (waxed) paper to allow space for the pudding to rise. Pour boiling water around the puddings to start them off well, and cook them on High.

◇ When adapting your own recipes, remember that fruit will require less cooking liquid.

ORANGE RICE PUDDING

—— SERVES 6 ——

✕	METRIC	IMPERIAL	AMERICAN
Butter or margarine	25 g	1 oz	2 tbsp
Milk	900 ml	1½ pts	3¾ cups
Evaporated milk	150 ml	¼ pt	⅔ cup
Short-grain pudding rice	100 g	4 oz	½ cup
Caster (superfine) sugar	50 g	2 oz	¼ cup
Grated rind and juice of orange	1	1	1
A few drops of vanilla essence (extract)			

① Butter the inside of the slo-cooker and preheat on High.

② Place all the ingredients into the slo-cooker and mix well.

③ Cook on Low for 6–8 hours.

—————— COOKING TIME: **LOW 6-8 HOURS** ——————

ALMOND RHUBARB PUDDING

—— SERVES 4 ——

✖	METRIC	IMPERIAL	AMERICAN
Butter or margarine, plus extra for greasing	100 g	4 oz	½ cup
Rhubarb, cut into 2.5 cm/1 in pieces	450 g	1 lb	1 lb
Caster (superfine) sugar	45 ml	3 tbsp	3 tbsp
Soft brown sugar	100 g	4 oz	½ cup
Eggs, beaten	2	2	2
Almond essence (extract)	10 ml	2 tsp	2 tsp
Self-raising (self-rising) flour	175 g	6 oz	1½ cups
Cocoa (unsweetened chocolate) powder	15 ml	1 tbsp	1 tbsp
Grated nutmeg	5 ml	1 tsp	1 tsp

① Lightly grease the inside of the slo-cooker, then preheat on High.

② Arrange the rhubarb in the base of the slo-cooker and sprinkle with the caster sugar.

③ Cream together the butter or margarine and brown sugar until light and fluffy. Gradually beat in the eggs and almond essence. Mix together the flour, cocoa and nutmeg, then fold into the mixture. Spread the mixture over the rhubarb and cover gently with a piece of buttered greaseproof (waxed) paper, buttered-side down.

④ Cook on High for 3–4 hours.

——————COOKING TIME: **HIGH 3–4 HOURS**——————

GOOSEBERRY PIE WITH WALNUTS

—— SERVES 4 ——

✗	METRIC	IMPERIAL	AMERICAN
Gooseberries	350 g	12 oz	12 oz
Butter, for greasing			
Caster (superfine) sugar	50 g	2 oz	¼ cup
Walnuts, chopped	25 g	1 oz	¼ cup
For the topping:			
Self-raising (self-rising) flour	100 g	4 oz	1 cup
Shredded suet	50 g	2 oz	½ cup
Caster (superfine) sugar	25 g	1 oz	2 tbsp
Milk	60 ml	4 tbsp	4 tbsp
Whipped cream and a few chopped walnuts, to decorate			

① Preheat the slo-cooker on High.

② Arrange the gooseberries in a lightly buttered ovenproof dish that fits inside the slo-cooker. Arrange the gooseberries in the dish and sprinkle with the sugar and walnuts.

③ To make the topping, mix together the flour, suet and sugar. Mix in the milk to make a firm dough. Roll out on a lightly floured board to a round that fits the dish. Lay the dough on the gooseberries and cover with buttered foil. Stand the dish in the slo-cooker and surround with sufficient boiling water to come half-way up the sides of the dish.

④ Cook on High for 3–4 hours.

⑤ Serve decorated with whipped cream and walnuts.

APRICOT BREAD AND BUTTER PUDDING
—— SERVES 4–6 ——

✗	METRIC	IMPERIAL	AMERICAN
Thin slices of bread, crusts removed	8	8	8
Butter or margarine, plus extra for greasing	25 g	1 oz	2 tbsp
Can of apricots, drained	400 g	14 oz	1 large
Caster (superfine) sugar	30 ml	2 tbsp	2 tbsp
Eggs, beaten	3	3	3
A few drops of almond essence (extract)			
Milk	450 ml	¾ pt	2 cups

① Preheat the slo-cooker on High.

② Spread the bread with the butter and cut into convenient-sized pieces to fit into your chosen dish. Use about three-quarters of the bread, buttered-side down, to line an ovenproof dish that fits inside the slo-cooker.

③ Reserve a few apricots for decoration, then chop the remainder finely and spread over the bread. Arrange the remaining bread slices on top.

④ Beat together the sugar, eggs and almond essence.

⑤ Warm the milk to lukewarm, then pour on to the eggs. Pour over the bread. Cover securely with buttered foil, then stand the dish in the slo-cooker and surround with sufficient boiling water to come half-way up the sides of the dish.

⑥ Cook on Low for 4–6 hours.

⑦ Decorate the pudding with the reserved apricots before serving.

—————— COOKING TIME: **LOW 4–6 HOURS** ——————

LEMON SPONGE WITH ALMONDS
—— SERVES 4 ——

✂ ❄

	METRIC	IMPERIAL	AMERICAN
Plain (all-purpose) flour	50 g	2 oz	½ cup
Baking powder	2.5 ml	½ tsp	½ tsp
Ground cinnamon	2.5 ml	½ tsp	½ tsp
Quick-cook rolled oats	50 g	2 oz	½ cup
Almonds, chopped	30 ml	2 tbsp	2 tbsp
Butter or margarine, plus extra for greasing	75 g	3 oz	⅓ cup
Soft brown sugar	100 g	4 oz	½ cup
Egg, beaten	1	1	1
Grated rind and juice of lemon	1	1	1
Milk	30 ml	2 tbsp	2 tbsp

① Preheat the slo-cooker on High.

② Mix together the flour, baking powder and cinnamon. Stir in the oats and almonds.

③ Beat together the butter and sugar until light and fluffy.

④ Lightly mix together the egg, lemon rind and 15 ml/ 1 tbsp of the lemon juice, then beat into the butter mixture a little at a time. Fold in the flour, then add enough of the milk to make a soft, dropping consistency.

⑤ Spoon the mixture into a buttered 600 ml/1 pt/2½ cup pudding basin and cover with lightly buttered foil. Stand the basin in the slo-cooker and surround with sufficient boiling water to come half-way up the sides of the basin.

⑥ Cook on High for 6–8 hours.

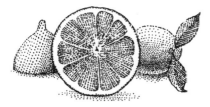

—— COOKING TIME: **HIGH 6–8 HOURS** ——

GINGERED RHUBARB

—— SERVES 4 ——

✗	METRIC	IMPERIAL	AMERICAN
Rhubarb, cut into 2.5 cm/1 in lengths	450 g	1 lb	1 lb
Water	150 ml	¼ pt	⅔ cup
Caster (superfine) sugar	60 ml	4 tbsp	4 tbsp
Grated rind and juice of orange	1	1	1
Whipped cream, to serve			
Preserved stem ginger in syrup, thinly sliced, to serve	15 ml	1 tbsp	1 tbsp

①   Preheat the slo-cooker on High.

②   Place all the ingredients in the slo-cooker and mix together well.

③   Cook on Low for 4–6 hours.

④   Transfer to a serving dish and chill until ready to serve.

⑤   Serve chilled, decorated with whipped cream and the ginger slices.

SYRUP PUDDING

—— SERVES 4 ——

✗	METRIC	IMPERIAL	AMERICAN
Self-raising (self-rising) flour	100 g	4 oz	1 cup
A pinch of salt			
Caster (superfine) sugar	50 g	2 oz	¼ cup
Shredded suet	50 g	2 oz	½ cup
Egg, beaten	1	1	1
Milk	45 ml	3 tbsp	3 tbsp
Butter, for greasing			
Golden (light corn) syrup	60 ml	4 tbsp	4 tbsp

① Preheat the slo-cooker on High.

② Mix together the flour, salt, sugar and suet. Stir in the egg and enough of the milk to make a soft, dropping consistency. Spoon the syrup into a buttered 600 ml/ 1 pt/2½ cup pudding basin, then carefully top with the sponge mixture and cover with buttered foil. Stand the basin in the slo-cooker and surround with sufficient boiling water to come half-way up the sides of the basin.

③ Cook on High for 3–4 hours.

④ Invert on to a warmed serving dish to serve.

————COOKING TIME: **HIGH 3–4 HOURS**————

BAKED APPLES WITH FRUIT AND NUT STUFFING

—— SERVES 4 ——

✄	METRIC	IMPERIAL	AMERICAN
Cooking (tart) apples	4	4	4
Raisins	25 g	1 oz	3 tbsp
Sultanas (golden raisins)	25 g	1 oz	3 tbsp
Soft brown sugar	50 g	2 oz	¼ cup
Hazelnuts (filberts), chopped	15 ml	1 tbsp	1 tbsp
A pinch of ground cinnamon			
Water	75 ml	5 tbsp	5 tbsp

① Preheat the slo-cooker on High.

② Core the apples and peel a strip around the 'equator' of each apple.

③ Mix together the raisins, sultanas, sugar, hazelnuts and cinnamon and press into the centres of the apples, piling any extra on top. Place the apples in the slo-cooker and spoon the water around.

④ Cook on Low for 4–6 hours.

—— COOKING TIME: **LOW 4–6 HOURS** ——

CHRISTMAS PUDDING

—— SERVES 6 ——

✗	METRIC	IMPERIAL	AMERICAN
Plain (all-purpose) flour	50 g	2 oz	½ cup
Mixed (apple-pie) spice	2.5 ml	½ tsp	½ tsp
Ground cinnamon	2.5 ml	½ tsp	½ tsp
Grated nutmeg	2.5 ml	½ tsp	½ tsp
Fresh breadcrumbs	50 g	2 oz	I cup
Shredded suet	150 g	5 oz	1¼ cups
Soft brown sugar	100 g	4 oz	½ cup
Raisins	175 g	6 oz	I cup
Sultanas (golden raisins)	175 g	6 oz	I cup
Chopped mixed (candied) peel	25 g	I oz	3 tbsp
Ground almonds	25 g	I oz	¼ cup
Large eggs, beaten	2	2	2
Finely grated rind and juice of orange	I	I	I
Black treacle (molasses)	15 ml	I tsp	I tbsp
Brandy or dry sherry	15 ml	I tbsp	I tbsp
Almond essence (extract)	2.5 ml	½ tsp	½ tsp
Beer	60 ml	4 tbsp	4 tbsp
Butter, for greasing			

① Preheat the slo-cooker on High.

② Mix all the dry ingredients. Beat the eggs with the remaining ingredients, then stir well into the flour mixture. Spoon the mixture into a buttered 1 litre/1¾ pt/ 4¼ cup pudding basin and cover securely with buttered foil. Stand the basin in the slo-cooker and surround with boiling water to come half-way up the sides of the basin.

③ Cook on High for 12 hours.

Reheating tip: Ideally, make your Christmas pudding in October and then leave to mature in a cool, dark place. To serve, preheat the slo-cooker on High for 20 minutes. Place the pudding in the slo-cooker and surround with boiling water, as before. Cook on Low for about 6 hours, or on High for about 4 hours.

—— COOKING TIME: **HIGH 12 HOURS** ——

BAKED CUSTARD
—— SERVES 4 ——

✖	METRIC	IMPERIAL	AMERICAN
Eggs	4	4	4
Caster (superfine) sugar	50 g	2 oz	¼ cup
Milk	600 ml	1 pt	2½ cups
A few drops of vanilla essence (extract)			
Grated nutmeg			

① Preheat the slo-cooker on High.

② Blend together the eggs and sugar.

③ Warm the milk to lukewarm, then pour on to the eggs and add the vanilla essence. Pour the custard into a 1 litre/1¾ pt/4¼ cup ovenproof dish and sprinkle with nutmeg, then cover with foil. Stand the dish in the slo-cooker and surround with sufficient boiling water to come half-way up the sides of the dish.

④ Cook on Low for 4–6 hours until a knife inserted in the centre comes out clean.

CRÈME CARAMEL

—— SERVES 4–6 ——

⚠	METRIC	IMPERIAL	AMERICAN
Caster (superfine) sugar	100 g	4 oz	½ cup
Water	150 ml	¼ pt	⅔ cup
Milk	600 ml	1 pt	2½ cups
Eggs	4	4	4
A few drops of vanilla essence (extract)			

① Preheat the slo-cooker on High.

② To make the caramel, heat 30 ml/2 tbsp of the sugar with the water in a small pan until the sugar has dissolved. Bring to the boil, then boil rapidly until it turns golden. Pour into a warmed soufflé dish and allow to cool.

③ Beat together the milk, eggs, vanilla essence and remaining sugar. Bring to blood heat, then strain on to the caramel. Cover with foil, then stand the dish in the slo-cooker and surround with sufficient boiling water to come half-way up the sides of the dish.

④ Cook on Low for 5–6 hours. Cooking times may vary depending on the type and size of dish used. The cooked custard should be just firm and set.

⑤ Leave to cool, then chill for several hours. Ease the custard away from the sides of the dish before turning out to serve.

—— COOKING TIME: **LOW 5–6 HOURS** ——

SLO-COOKED GINGERBREAD

—— SERVES 8–10 ——

✂ ✳	METRIC	IMPERIAL	AMERICAN
Dark Muscovado sugar	225 g	8 oz	1 cup
Butter or margarine, plus extra for greasing	175 g	6 oz	¾ cup
Golden (light corn) syrup	350 g	12 oz	1 cup
Plain (all-purpose) flour	450 g	1 lb	1 lb
Salt	5 ml	1 tsp	1 tsp
Ground ginger	15 ml	1 tbsp	1 tbsp
Baking powder	10 ml	2 tsp	2 tsp
Egg	1	1	1
Milk	300 ml	½ pt	1¼ cups
Glacé (candied) cherries, chopped, or chopped mixed (candied) peel	50 g	2 oz	⅓ cup
Caster (superfine) sugar	50 g	2 oz	¼ cup
Water	30 ml	2 tbsp	2 tbsp

① Preheat the slo-cooker on High.

② Melt together the Muscovado sugar, butter or margarine and syrup gently in a non-stick pan until the sugar has dissolved. Allow to cool.

③ Place the flour, salt, ginger and baking powder in a bowl and make a well in the centre. Pour in the melted mixture, the egg and milk and mix until smooth. Pour into a buttered 18 cm/ 7 in round cake tin (pan) and sprinkle with the chopped glacé cherries or mixed peel. Cover with buttered foil and stand the tin in the slo-cooker. Surround with sufficient boiling water to come half-way up the sides of the tin.

④ Cook on High for 6–8 hours.

⑤ Turn the gingerbread out of the tin. Blend together the caster sugar and water and brush over the top of the hot gingerbread. Leave to cool.

Freezing tip: Interleave slices of gingerbread with greaseproof (waxed) paper and wrap securely in foil to freeze so you can use individual servings.

—————— COOKING TIME: **HIGH 6–8 HOURS** ——————

NUT AND BANANA BREAD

—— SERVES 6–8 ——

	METRIC	IMPERIAL	AMERICAN
Self-raising (self-rising) flour	175 g	6 oz	1½ cups
A pinch of salt			
Grated nutmeg	2.5 ml	½ tsp	½ tsp
Butter or margarine, plus extra for greasing	75 g	3 oz	⅓ cup
Muscovado sugar	100 g	4 oz	½ cup
Sultanas (golden raisins)	50 g	2 oz	⅓ cup
Chopped mixed nuts	50 g	2 oz	½ cup
Ripe bananas, chopped	3	3	3
Eggs, beaten	2	2	2

①　Preheat the slo-cooker on High.

②　Mix together the flour, salt and nutmeg in a bowl, then rub in the butter or margarine until the mixture resembles breadcrumbs. Stir in the sugar, sultanas and nuts.

③　Mash the bananas until soft, then stir into the eggs. Mix into the dry ingredients until well blended. Spoon into a buttered 18 cm/7 in cake tin (pan) and cover with foil. Place in the slo-cooker and surround with sufficient boiling water to come half-way up the sides of the tin.

④　Cook on High for 2–3 hours.

⑤　Serve sliced and buttered.

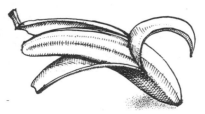

—————— COOKING TIME: **HIGH 2–3 HOURS** ——————

CHOCOLATE CAKE WITH BUTTER ICING

—— SERVES 6–8 ——

✕ ❄

	METRIC	IMPERIAL	AMERICAN
For the cake:			
Cocoa (unsweetened chocolate) powder	15 ml	1 tbsp	1 tbsp
Hot water	30 ml	2 tbsp	2 tbsp
Butter or margarine, plus extra for greasing	100 g	4 oz	½ cup
Caster (superfine) sugar	100 g	4 oz	½ cup
Eggs, beaten	2	2	2
Self-raising (self-rising) flour	100 g	4 oz	1 cup
For the icing (frosting):			
Cocoa powder	30 ml	2 tbsp	2 tbsp
Hot water	30 ml	2 tbsp	2 tbsp
Icing (confectioners') sugar	225 g	8 oz	1⅓ cups
Butter or margarine, softened	75 g	3 oz	⅓ cup
Milk	45 ml	3 tbsp	3 tbsp

① Preheat the slo-cooker on High.

② To make the cake, blend the cocoa to a paste with the hot water, then leave to cool.

③ Cream together the butter or margarine and sugar until light and fluffy. Beat in the cocoa mixture, then beat in the eggs a little at a time alternately with a little of the flour. Gently fold in the remaining flour. Spoon the mixture into a buttered 18 cm/7 in cake tin (pan) and cover with foil. Stand the tin in the slo-cooker and surround with sufficient boiling water to come half-way up the sides of the tin.

④ Cook on High for 3–4 hours.

⑤ To make the icing, blend the cocoa and hot water to a paste, then leave to cool.

⑥ Gradually beat the icing sugar and cocoa mixture into the butter or margarine, adding enough of the milk to make a smooth but fairly stiff butter icing.

⑦ Halve the cooled cake horizontally, then sandwich together with half the icing. Spread the remaining icing on top.

COOKING TIME: **HIGH 3–4 HOURS**

PINEAPPLE UPSIDE-DOWN CAKE
—— SERVES 4 ——

	METRIC	IMPERIAL	AMERICAN
Butter or margarine	50 g	2 oz	¼ cup
Soft brown sugar	100 g	4 oz	½ cup
Can of pineapple slices, drained	400 g	14 oz	1 large
A few glacé (candied) cherries			
For the sponge:			
Butter or margarine	175 g	6 oz	¾ cup
Caster (superfine) sugar	175 g	6 oz	¾ cup
Eggs, beaten	3	3	3
Self-raising (self-rising) flour	175 g	6 oz	1½ cups
Milk	130 ml	2 tbsp	2 tbsp

① Place the butter or margarine in the slo-cooker to melt and preheat on High.

② Stir in the sugar, then arrange the pineapple slices and cherries over the base of the dish.

③ To make the sponge, cream together the butter or margarine and sugar, then gradually beat in the eggs, a little at a time, and fold in the flour. Add enough of the milk to make a soft, dropping consistency. Spoon the sponge mixture over the pineapple and topping.

④ Cook on High for 1 hour, then Low for 3–4 hours.

⑤ Turn out and serve warm as a dessert or cold as a cake.

COOKING TIME: **HIGH 1 HOUR, THEN LOW 3-4 HOURS**

INDEX